Reading English Discourse

Reading English Discourse

business, economics, law, and political science

LYLE F. BACHMAN
University of Illinois

Prentice-Hall, Inc. Englewood Cliffs, NJ 07632

Library of Congress Cataloging in Publication Data

Bachman, Lyle F., (date)
Reading English Discourse.

1. College readers. 2. English language—Text-books for foreign speakers. 3. Readers—Social sciences. 4. Readers—Business. 5. Readers—Law. I. Title.
PE1122.B325 1986 428.6 85-6568
ISBN 0-13-755844-9

Editorial/production supervision and interior design by **Martha Masterson**
Cover design by **Diane Saxe**
Manufacturing buyer: **Harry P. Baisley**

Printed in the United States of America

10 9 8 7 6 5 4 3 2 1

ISBN 0-13-755844-9 01

Prentice-Hall International (UK) Limited, *London*
Prentice-Hall of Australia Pty. Limited, *Sydney*
Prentice-Hall Canada Inc., *Toronto*
Prentice-Hall Hispanoamericana, S. A., *Mexico*
Prentice-Hall of India Private Limited, *New Delhi*
Prentice-Hall of Japan, Inc., *Tokyo*
Prentice-Hall of Southeast Asia Pte. Ltd., *Singapore*
Editora Prentice-Hall do Brasil, Ltda., *Rio de Janeiro*
Whitehall Books Limited, *Wellington, New Zealand*

Contents

Unit II EXEMPLIFICATION

Unit IV DEFINITION

Unit V CAUSATION

Preface

Reading English Discourse is aimed at developing the reading skills of upper intermediate university and preuniversity students who need English as a tool for reading professional materials in their own chosen disciplines. The core learning objectives are text-level discourse and rhetorical functions and vocabulary skills rather than sentence-level grammar. At the same time, the structures typically associated with given discourse functions are an integral part of each lesson. This text was written for students from all language backgrounds, whose native language is not English, although it may also be used by native English-speaking students who would like to improve their reading skills.

The *Teacher's Guide* to this text contains descriptions of the materials and their objectives, suggestions for teaching, answers to the exercises, and supplemental exercises. The *Teacher's Guide* will be particularly useful to those teachers who may have a minimal background in the fields of business, economics, law, and political science.

It has been my experience that the majority of university- and preuniversity-level students have been taught the major sentence-level grammatical structures of English, but may not have learned how these sentence structures are used to form larger units of discourse—paragraphs and whole texts. Likewise, they may already have learned a fairly large number of "general" vocabulary items. For such students, the major difficulties in reading formal academic English are likely to be in recognizing how the grammatical structures they have learned are used to signal a wide range of discourse meanings, in comprehending new vocabulary items which are characteristic of academic

English, and in discovering the specific meanings individual words may take on in the context of a reading passage. For these reasons, the focus of this book is not on grammatical structures, but on the organization of discourse and on the development of vocabulary and vocabulary skills.

These materials had their beginning in a cooperative project between the Division of English as a Second Language, University of Illinois at Urbana-Champaign and the Tehran University Language Center. That project provided the research basis for these materials: the identification of specific disciplines related to the major fields of interest, the lexical analysis of representative texts from these disciplines, and a review of the research and materials then available in the field of English for Specific Purposes. The early units (I–III) were also written, tried out, and evaluated as part of this project. Due to the unexpected turn of events in Iran, it was not possible to complete the materials there; the rewriting of the early units and the writing of the final two units was completed by the author in Illinois.

I would like to thank the following individuals and organizations: Dr. Mehri Ahy, formerly director of the Tehran University Language Center, and Robert Rogers, formerly dean of the College of Liberal Arts and Sciences, University of Illinois, as well as Tehran University and the University of Illinois at Urbana-Champaign, for their support of the original materials development project; John Kostovich and Dick Russell, who assisted in the initial research; Jackie Amirhor, Aghdas Dastguib, Mike Lipinski, Pat Owens, Mersedeh Noormohamadian Proctor, Ed Weidhmann, and Carol Zehren, who also assisted in the research and who wrote the early units; Linda Reingardt, who wrote some materials in the early units and who assisted greatly in their revision; the many students and teachers at the Tehran University Language Center, who tried out and gave us feedback on the materials; Linda Blanton and Grace Burkart, for their valuable comments; and Jean Brown who provided assistance in biographic research.

Lyle F. Bachman

Champaign, Illinois

Credits

p. 4 from Joel Larus, ed., *Comparative World Politics* (Belmont, California: Wadsworth Publishing Co., 1966), pp. 3–4, 18, 144–145.

p. 16 Freely Adapted from T. N. Dupuy and G. M. Hammerman, eds., *A Documentary History of Arms Control and Disarmament* (New York: T. N. Dupuy Associates, 1973), p. 13.

p. 22 Original passage, Edward Wiedhmann, 1977.

p. 32 Original passage, Edward Wiedhmann, 1977.

p. 37 Reprinted with permission of Macmillan Publishing Co., from *The World's Police* by James Cramer, originally published by Cassel & Co. Ltd.)

p. 48 Reprinted with permission of Macmillan Publishing Co., from *The World's Police* by James Cramer, originally published by Cassel & Co. Ltd.)

p. 62 from Wayne G. Broehl, Jr., *Trucks, Trouble and Triumph: The Norwalk Truck Line Company,* © 1954. Adapted by permission of Prentice-Hall, Inc., Englewood Cliffs, NJ.

p. 68 from Paul A. Samuelson, *Economics,* 8th ed. (New York: McGraw-Hill) pp. 86–87.
p. 79 from Paul A. Samuelson, *Economics,* 8th ed. (New York: McGraw-Hill) pp. 86–87.
p. 84 from Carl H. Madden, "Why We Must Have Industrial Growth," *Nation's Business* March 1976, pp. 38, 44. Copyright 1976, Chamber of Commerce of the United States.
p. 97 from Carl H. Madden, "Why We Must Have Industrial Growth," *Nation's Business* March 1976, pp. 38, 44. Copyright 1976, Chamber of Commerce of the United States.
p. 102 Adapted from Geoffrey Whitehead, *Economics Made Simple* (London: William Heinemann Ltd.), 1982, pp. 26–28, 184–185.
p. 114 Adapted from Geoffrey Whitehead, *Economics Made Simple* (London: William Heinemann Ltd.), 1982, pp.·26–28, 184–185.
p. 118 Adapted from Geoffrey Whitehead, *Economics Made Simple* (London: William Heinemann Ltd.), 1982, pp. 26–28, 184–185.
p. 130 Adapted from Geoffrey Whitehead, *Economics Made Simple* (London: William Heinemann Ltd.), 1982, pp. 26–28, 184–185.
p. 133 from Raymond Vernon, "Multinational Enterprise and National Security," *Adelphi Papers* No. 4 74 (January 1971), pp. 4, 8–9.
p. 148 from Raymond Vernon, "Multinational Enterprise and National Security," *Adelphi Papers* No. 4 74 (January 1971), pp. 4, 8–9.
p. 163 from John C. Meyer, Jr., "Reporting Crime in the Press," *Criminology* 14, no. 2 (August 1976), 277–278.
p. 172 Original passage, Edward Wiedhmann, 1978.
p. 176 from John P. Alston, "Japanese and American Attitudes toward the Abolition of Capital Punishment," *Criminology,* 14 no. 2 (August 1976) 274–275.
p. 189 from L. Broom and P. Selznick, *Sociology: A Text with Adapted Readings* (New York: Harper & Row Publishers, Inc., 1968), pp. 423–424.
p. 193 Adapted from *Human Behavior: Shorter Edition* by Bernard Berelson and Gary A. Steiner, copyright © 1967 by Harcourt Brace Jovanovich, Inc. Reprinted by permission of the publisher.
p. 202 Adapted from *Human Behavior: Shorter Edition* by Bernard Berelson and Gary A. Steiner, copyright © 1967 by Harcourt Brace Jovanovich, Inc. Reprinted by permission of the publisher.
p. 219 from Joel Larus, ed., *Comparative World Politics* (Belmont, California: Wadsworth Publishing Co., 1966), pp. 3–4, 18, 144–145.
p. 228 from Dorothy M. Pickles, *Introduction to Politics.* (London: Sylvan Press, 1967), pp. 84–86.
p. 232 from Henry Jacoby, *The Bureaucratization of the World* (Berkeley, California: University of California Press, 1973), pp. 197–198.
p. 242 from Henry Jacoby, *The Bureaucratization of the World* (Berkeley, California: University of California Press, 1973), pp. 197–198.
p. 246 from Paul A. Samuelson, *Economics,* 8th ed. (New York: McGraw-Hill), pp. 86–87.
p. 259 from Paul A. Samuelson, *Economics,* 8th ed. (New York: McGraw-Hill), pp. 86–87.
p. 263 from *Sociology: The Study of Human Interaction, Revised Edition,* by David Dressler with Donald Carns. Copyright © 1969 by David Dressler. Copyright © 1973 by Alfred A. Knopf, Inc. Reprinted by permission of the publisher.
p. 276 from *Sociology: The Study of Human Interaction, Revised Edition,* by David Dressler with Donald Carns. Copyright © 1969 by David Dressler. Copyright © 1973 by Alfred A. Knopf, Inc. Reprinted by permission of the publisher.

Reading English Discourse

Introduction

If you look at the Table of Contents of this book, you will probably recognize some familiar components, such as "Reading Passages," "Comprehension Exercises," "Vocabulary Exercises," and "Word Skills." At the same time, you may wonder what "Discourse Skills" are, and why there are no "grammar" or "structure" exercises. When you use language for communication, such as when you read a textbook or a journal article in your field, you are not interested so much in what structures the author uses, as in his or her intended meaning. In discourse, where sentences are combined into paragraphs and whole passages, grammatical structures are used to express or signal different meanings and relationships among the ideas expressed, and individual words take on different, more specialized meanings. To understand the meaning of an entire text, therefore, you must be able to follow the organization of the discourse, using grammatical structures and words as signals of the author's meaning.

These materials are designed to help you apply the knowledge of English sentences and vocabulary that you already have to the understanding of the organization of discourse in reading passages. They will also help you extend your knowledge of vocabulary by showing you how to use information in the context of reading passages to discover the meaning of new words. The book contains five units—"Time Order," "Exemplification," "Comparison and Contrast," "Definition," and "Causation"—each dealing with a major discourse function. The lessons in each unit are based on reading passages related to the fields of business, economics, law, and political science. While you may learn something about these fields from the readings, the main purpose is to help you learn the discourse structures and vocabulary that are typical of writings in these fields.

Each lesson begins with "Prereading Exercises," which are to be done before reading the passage. The "Discussion Questions" are aimed at introducing the topic of the reading and at getting you to think about some of the ideas discussed in the reading passage. The words defined in the "Special Vocabulary" are words you will need to know in order to understand the reading passage. Next, there are some "Guide Questions" that will help you to focus your reading on specific kinds of information.

The next part of each lesson includes two versions of the same reading passage. "Passage A" is a simplified version, which you should be able to read and comprehend easily. "Passage B" is more like the original text and includes the rhetorical structures and vocabulary that will be taught in the lesson. The words in "Passage B" which are **boldfaced** have nearly the same meaning as the corresponding **boldfaced** words or phrases in "Passage A." You should read "Passage A" first and then answer the "Guide Questions," either orally or in writing. Then you should read "Passage B," referring back to "Passage A" as necessary to find the meanings of any words you may not know.

Next, there are several exercises which are based on "Passage B." The "Comprehension Exercises" are aimed at helping you to understand the meaning of certain parts of the passage and to identify certain parts of the discourse organization of the passage. The "Vocabulary Exercises" are aimed at helping you to learn the meanings of words that are frequently used in the fields of business, economics, law, and political science. The "Word Skills" exercises are aimed at helping you to recognize and understand the meanings of the affixes that are used in English to form new words. In the "Discourse Skills" exercises, you will analyze the discourse organization of "Passage B" and will sometimes review grammatical structures that are used to signal that organization.

The final part of each unit is a "Reading Exercise," which includes a short passage related to the topic of lesson and which will enable you to develop your skills in using the context of the passage to discover the meaning of new words.

Lesson 1

Power Politics in Ancient China

PREREADING ACTIVITIES

A. Discussion Questions

1. What do you think about when you hear the word *ancient?*
2. What ancient events or people do you know about?
3. What is an empire?
4. What empires do you know about?

B. Special Vocabulary (Marked "*" in Passage A)

power politics	the policies or affairs of a government that enable it to control or influence other nations
nation-state	a form of government consisting of several groups of people or tribes organized under a single government
dynasty	a succession of rulers from the same family or line which controls power for several generations
tribe	a social organization consisting of several villages or other groups sharing a common language, culture, and name

culture	the arts, beliefs, institutions, and patterns of behaving that are qualities of a group of people
tributary system	a social, economic, and political network that requires the payment of money or goods by one nation to another

C. Guide Questions

As you read Passage A, ask yourself the following questions:

1. Who is thought to understand ancient Chinese history?
2. Did the ancient Chinese know about power politics?
3. What must we look at to understand that the Chinese knew about power politics?
4. When did China become a great power?
5. Who affected the thinking of the Chinese of the fifth century B.C.?
6. On what two ideas was China's tributary system based?
7. How long did the tributary system last?
8. What did the tributary system allow neighboring countries to do?

NOW READ PASSAGE A. WHEN YOU FINISH READING, ANSWER THE GUIDE QUESTIONS.

READING PASSAGES

Power Politics in Ancient China

Adapted from Joel Larus, 1966

Passage A

It is a common **unproven belief** that the ancient Far East is **difficult** to understand. It is thought that only **people with special knowledge** of this area understand its ancient history. Because of this, many students think that this non-Western area did not know about *power politics before the time when **people from Europe** went there **to live** or **to buy and sell.** If we look at the system which existed **between** the **states** controlled by the Chinese Empire, we will find that this idea is not **true.** The Chinese did know about power politics. For example, centuries before the **time** of the *nation-state[1] China

[1]The time, beginning in the sixteenth century A.D., when small independent states were brought together to form nations. In the Christian calendar, dates before the birth of Christ are written "B.C."; dates after the birth of Christ are written "A.D."

had become a great power. This great power also controlled a **large** part of the world.

At the time of the *Shang Dynasty,[2] the Chinese began to develop a new plan for **directing** the **business** they did with their neighbors. During the centuries of **meeting** with these neighboring *tribes and states, the Chinese felt **sure** that they were much better in *culture, behavior, and the way their government was organized. Later, in the fifth century B.C., the Chinese were **affected** by the teachings of their great teacher and philosopher, Confucius. His ideas on government included **governing** by good example, **acting politely,** and trying not to use force to solve the problems of **government.**

China's famous *tributary system was **built upon** these teachings of Confucius and the belief that they, the Chinese, were culturally better than their neighbors. This tributary system between China and its neighbors continued for hundreds of years. During these centuries, Peking expected its **uncultured** neighbors to send representatives and **gifts** to the emperor **often and at regular times.** Because of this system, the neighboring countries wanted to become part of the Chinese Empire. The tributary system allowed them to do this.

NOW GO BACK AND ANSWER THE GUIDE QUESTIONS.

Passage B

An **assumption** is commonly made that the ancient Far East is **impossible** to understand to anyone but area **experts.** The result is that many students have the idea that this non-Western area did not know about power politics before the first **European settlers** and **traders** arrived. If we look at the **interstate** system of the Chinese Empire, we will see that this is not a **realistic** point of view. Centuries before the **age** of the nation-state (sixteenth century A.D.), China in its own way had become a great power which controlled a **significant** area of the world.

As early as the Shang Dynasty (1766–1123 B.C.), the Chinese began to develop a plan for **conducting relations** with neighboring tribes and states. During centuries of **contact** with their neighbors, the Chinese became **certain** that they were greatly **superior** in culture, behavior, and governmental organization. Later, in the fifth century B.C., the Chinese were **influenced** by the teachings of their great teacher and philosopher, Confucius. His ideas on government included **ruling** by good example, **politeness,** and trying not to use force to solve **political** problems.

The belief that they were culturally superior and the teachings of Confucius were the **foundation** of China's famous tributary system. This was an interstate system that continued for hundreds of years. During these centuries, Peking expected its **uncivilized** neighbors **periodically** to send repre-

[2]Shang Dynasty (1766–1123 B.C.) An important royal family in ancient China.

sentatives and **presents** to the emperor. This system provided a desire and a way for the once uncivilized countries to become part of the very civilized Chinese world.

COMPREHENSION EXERCISES

Exercise 1

The adverb *before* introduces the second point in time.

Example: The Shang Dynasty existed before the time of Confucius.

First point in time (The Shang Dynasty) — Second point in time (the time of Confucius)

The adverb *after* introduces the first point in time.

Example: Confucius lived after the time of the Shang Dynasty.

Second point in time (Confucius lived) — First point in time (the time of the Shang Dynasty)

Read each sentence below. Find each time expression that begins with "before" or "after." Underline the *first* point in time, and draw *two lines* under the *second* point in time.

1. The Chinese, after centuries of contact with their neighbors, felt that they were superior.
2. It was years before the House of Han took power again.
3. After uniting their lands at home, the first Chinese emperors reopened the war with Korea.
4. Even before the 770s, a certain amount of literature was produced in China.
5. The Middle Ages began after the fall of Rome.
6. The state capitals were known for their production of cloth, salt, fish, and, after 500 B.C., iron.
7. Horseback riders were probably unknown in China before 350 B.C.
8. Before 300 B.C., the Chinese knew about the other Asian countries around them.
9. One prince set up capitals in a number of places before reaching Hanchow.

10. Genghis Khan captured the Chinese capital in 1215 A.D. after a terrifying battle.

Exercise 2

Reread the sentences in Exercise 1. Then number the events or points in time in each pair of sentences below, in the order in which they actually happened. Write "1" for the first event and "2" for the second event.

_______ 1. The Chinese felt they were superior.
_______ The Chinese had centuries of contact with their neighbors.
_______ 2. Years passed.
_______ The House of Han took power again.
_______ 3. The first Chinese emperors united their lands at home.
_______ The first Chinese emperors reopened the war with Korea.
_______ 4. The 770s.
_______ A certain amount of literature was produced in China.
_______ 5. The Middle Ages began.
_______ Rome fell.
_______ 6. The state capitals were known for their production of iron.
_______ 500 B.C.
_______ 7. Horseback riders were unknown in China.
_______ 350 B.C.
_______ 8. The Chinese knew about the other Asian countries.
_______ 300 B.C.
_______ 9. One prince set up capitals in many places.
_______ One prince reached Hanchow.
_______ 10. There was a terrifying battle.
_______ Genghis Khan captured the Chinese capital.

Exercise 3

Reread Passage B and answer the following questions:

1. In line 3, *this non-Western area* refers to ______________________
____.

2. In line 5, *this* refers to ____

____.

3. In line 12, *they* refers to ____.
4. In line 14, *his* refers to ____.
5. In line 17, *the teachings* refers to ____

____.

6. In line 18, *this* refers to ____

____.

7. In lines 19–20 *these centuries* refers to ____

____.

8. In line 21, *this system* means ____

____.

VOCABULARY EXERCISES

Exercise 4

Fill in the blanks with words from the list. Each word is used only once.

assumption	experts	periodically
conducting	foundation	relations
contact	interstate	significant
certain		

Many students of the ancient Far East make an ________________ that the subject is impossible to understand. They have the idea that the Chinese of that time did not know about power politics. ________________ tell us, however, that China controlled a ________________ part of the ancient Far East and was a great power. During hundreds of years of ________________ with their neighbors, the Chinese became ________________ that they were superior to their neighbors and made them send representatives and gifts ________________ to the Chinese emperor. The idea that they were superior and the teachings of Confucius were the ________________________ of China's famous tributary system. This was the ________________________ plan that the Chinese developed for ________________________ ________________________ with their neighbors.

Exercise 5

Choose the word from the list that has nearly the same meaning as the phrase in parentheses, and use it to complete the sentence.

assumption	expert	periodically
conducting	foundation	relations
contact	interstate	significant
certain		

1. (A person with a lot of special skill or knowledge) An ________________________ is a person who has a special knowledge about a subject such as the ancient Far East.
2. (between two or more states) The ________________________ relations between the Chinese Empire and neighboring tribes was unusual.
3. (when something is repeated at regular times) The Chinese emperor ________________________ received presents.
4. (coming together with someone or something) The Chinese had hundreds of years of ________________________ with their neighbors.
5. (very sure about something) The ancient Chinese were ________________________ that their neighbors were not as clever as they were.
6. (that upon which something is built) The teachings of Confucius were the ________________________ of centuries of Chinese political thinking.
7. (something that we suppose is true) Many people make the ________________________ that Chinese power politics began after contact with European settlers and traders.
8. (getting together to do something for business or politics) The Chinese began to develop a plan for conducting ________________________ with neighboring tribes and states very early in their history.
9. (very large or important) The Chinese Empire was a ________________________ part of the ancient Far East.

10. (directing something) The Chinese were clever at ______________ relations with their neighbors.

WORD SKILLS

A. The noun suffixes *-ion, -tion,* and *-ation*

Examples from Passage B: assump*tion* (l. 1)
founda*tion* (l. 18)

The suffixes *-ion, -tion,* and *-ation* are added to verbs to form nouns.

Examples:

Verbs	*Nouns*
express	expression
intend	intention*
produce	production*

*Note spelling change.

Exercise 6

Write the correct verb form of the underlined noun in each of the sentences below.

Example: Their description of the thief was very good.
They ___described___ the thief very well.

1. It is my assumption that taxes will go higher soon.
   I ______________ that taxes will go higher soon.
2. She will make a comparison of the prices at the two stores.
   She will ______________ the prices at the two stores.
3. We made the correction on their tests yesterday.
   We ______________ their tests yesterday.
4. Their conversation ended at 3 A.M.
   They ______________ until 3 A.M.
5. Our intention is to submit our plans next week.
   We ______________ to submit our plans next week.

B. The adjective suffix *-ic*

Example from Passage B: realist*ic* (l. 6)

The suffix *-ic* is usually added to nouns to form adjectives.

Examples: *Noun*	*Adjective*
base	*basic**
geography	*geographic**

*Note spelling change.

Exercise 7

Write the noun forms of the adjectives below.

Adjective	*Noun*
democratic	________________
photographic	________________
realistic	________________
symbolic	________________
telegraphic	________________

C. The adjective suffix *-al*

Example from Passage B: government*al* (l. 12)

The suffix *-al* is usually added to nouns to form adjectives.

Examples: *Noun*	*Adjective*
habit	habitual*
industry	industrial*
tradition	traditional

*Note spelling change.

Exercise 8

Write the adjective forms of the underlined nouns in the sentences below.

Example: John can perform music very well.
John is a ___musical___ person.

1. Prof. Jones did a study of the region.

   Prof. Jones did a ________________ study.
2. She works for an organization of the government.

   She works for a ________________ organization.

3. Phyllis received her experience through practice.

   Phyllis received ________________ experience.

4. The report from our government office in Tangiers has just arrived.

   The ________________ report from Tangiers has just arrived.

5. The government built a new factory as an experiment.

   The government built a new ________________ factory.

The suffix *-al* is also added to adjectives ending in *-ic* to form adjectives.

Examples:	*Adjective*	*Adjective*
	economic	economical
	geographic	geographical
	historic	historical

Sometimes there is a difference in meaning between adjectives ending in *-ic* and *-ical*.

Examples:	economic	having to do with handling money
	economical	being careful with money
	historic	famous in history
	historical	concerned with history

Exercise 9

Fill in the blanks below with the correct adjective form.

economy	1. Peter was a very ________________ person. He only spent money when it was absolutely necessary.
history	2. One of the most famous places in America is Boston. Boston is an ________________ place.
period	3. They received ________________ letters from their family in America.
type	4. It was a ________________ day; nothing unusual had happened.

economy 5. We assumed that this would be a very serious ________________ problem for our government.

D. The adverb suffix *-ly*

Examples from Passage B: common*ly* (l. 1)
great*ly* (l. 12)
periodical*ly* (l. 20)

The suffix *-ly* is usually added to adjectives to form adverbs.

Examples: *Adjective*	*Adverb*
economical	economically
regular	regularly

The suffix *-ly* is sometimes added to nouns to form adverbs of time.

Examples: *Noun*	*Adverb*
day	daily*
week	weekly

Write the adverb for the underlined adjectives or nouns in the sentences below.

Example: Jean is a <u>careful</u> driver.
Jean drives ____carefully____.

1. <u>Occasional</u> reports were sent to the main office, but we didn't think they were important.

   Reports were ________________ sent to the main office, but we didn't think they were important.
2. What was the <u>actual</u> amount you had to pay?

   What was the amount you ________________ had to pay?
3. It is <u>possible</u> that economic conditions will improve soon.

   Economic conditions will ________________ improve soon.
4. The <u>annual</u> rate of increase in the population is six percent.

   The population increases six percent ________________.
5. <u>The first thing</u> that must be done is to organize the reports to the president.

   ________________, the reports to the president must be organized.

DISCOURSE SKILLS

Exercise 11

Reread Passage B and complete the following.

1. The general time period of the passage is

   centuries before ______________________________

This phrase shows a *general time period.*

2. What had the Chinese become during this period?

   ____

3. The earliest *event* in the passage occurred

   As early as ______________________________

This phrase shows a *specific time period.*

4. The specific dates of the Shang Dynasty were

   ____

5. What did the Chinese do during this period?

   began to develop ______________________________

   ____

6. What did the Chinese have during this period?

   centuries ______________________________

7. What did the Chinese become during this period?

   certain that ______________________________

8. What is the next *specific time period* mentioned in the passage?

   Later, ______________________________

9. What influenced the Chinese at that time?

   ____

10. Was the period of China's tributary system before or after the period of Confucius?

    ____

11. What did the Chinese do during the time of their tributary system?

    controlled ______________________________

    expected ______________________________

These two conditions were *simultaneous*—during the same specific time period or at the same point in time.

Exercise 12

Number the following events or conditions in the order in which they actually happened in Chinese history, beginning with "1" for the first event. Give *simultaneous* events or conditions the same number.

_______ 1. The Chinese became certain that they were superior to their neighbors.

_______ 2. The Chinese were influenced by Confucius.

_______ 3. China controlled a significant area of the world.

_______ 4. The Chinese began to develop a plan for conducting relations with their neighbors.

_______ 5. The tributary system was used.

_______ 6. The Chinese had centuries of contact with neighboring tribes and states.

_______ 7. The age of the nation-state.

_______ 8. Peking expected gifts and representatives.

Exercise 13

In the accompanying time chart, fill in the blanks as follows:

1: General time period of Passage B
2–5: Specific time periods mentioned in Passage B
A–F: Things that the Chinese did during these specific time periods

	The Time of	*The Chinese*
16th Century A.D.	5. ____________________	
	____________________	
	4. ____________________	A. controlled ____________
		____________________
		B. expected ____________
		____________________
		____________________

Centuries before	5th Century B.C.	3. __________	C. were influenced __________ __________ __________ __________
1. _____ _____ _____ _____	1123 B.C.	2. __________	D. began __________ __________ E. had contact __________ __________ F. became certain __________ __________
	1766 B.C.		

READING EXERCISE

Adapted from T. N. Dupuy and G. M. Hammerman, 1973

Read the passage below and then do the exercises that follow.

Feudalism was dying in the fifteenth and sixteenth centuries, and the strong nation-state was taking the place of this old system of small, private states. These modern nation-states were well organized and could wage wars using many more soldiers than before. Because more soldiers were involved in the fighting, wars became bloodier and large armies were very common. Guns began to be used instead of other weapons, such as swords and spears. Before this, soldiers had worn suits made of metal which protected them against spears and swords. These suits of armor were expensive, so only rich people could fight wars. However, armor could not protect the soldier against firearms. Gunpowder, a substance used in all guns or firearms, therefore, became an important part of war. Wars were no longer fought by rich people with suits of armor. The common person, using firearms and gunpowder, became more important as a soldier. Thus, gunpowder helped to facilitate the transition from feudalism to the nation-state.

Vocabulary in Context

In the passage above there were probably several words that you did not know. The following is one method you can use to find the meaning of words from their **context.** You can ask questions about their grammatical position in the sentence (is it the subject? object?), about their part of speech (verb? noun?), and about other words in the passage that might mean the same thing.

"Feudalism" is a **noun.** We know this because the *-ism* ending is always used with nouns (*communism, capitalism,* etc.). It is the subject of the sentence. The verb "dying" describes what is happening to feudalism. "Feudalism" refers to events or conditions in the past. These conditions were economic, social, and political. To what other words does "feudalism" refer? The word "this" (line 2) tells us that "feudalism" refers to "old system of small, private states." We now have a definition of "feudalism."

Using this method, do the following exercises.

Exercise 14

In the blanks below, write the word from the passage that has nearly the same meaning as the **boldface** words and phrases in the following sentences.

1. The nation-state was taking the place of the **old system of small, private states.**

   ____

2. Gunpowder became an important part of fighting wars. Gunpowder helped **make** the transition from feudalism **much quicker and easier.**

   ____

3. The **change** from feudalism to the nation-state was facilitated by the use of gunpowder in fighting wars.

   ____

4. **Metal suits** could protect the soldier against spears and swords.

   ____

5. The modern nation-states were well organized and could **fight** wars using many more soldiers than before.

   ____

6. Because soldiers were **taking part** in these wars, the wars became much larger and bloodier.

   ____

7. The **substance that helps guns work** was important in bringing an end to feudalism.

   ____

8. **Guns** were used in wars after the discovery of gunpowder.

   ____

9. Guns also began to be used instead of other **instruments used to wage wars,** such as swords and spears.

   ____

Exercise 15

Read the following short passages and select the best answer for each from the choices given. Circle the letter for your choice.

1. Feudalism was dying in the fifteenth and sixteenth centuries. The strong nation-state was taking the place of this old system of small, private states.
   Feudalism probably means
   a. sixteenth century
   b. nation-state
   c. taking the place of
   d. system of small, private states
2. Gunpowder helped to facilitate the transition from feudalism to the nation-state. Without gunpowder, the transition might have been much slower and more difficult.
   Facilitate probably means
   a. to make slower
   b. gunpowder
   c. to make quicker and easier
   d. transition
3. The transition from feudalism to the nation-state was facilitated by gunpowder. As the system of government passed from one form to another, the lives of the people were changed.
   Transition means
   a. system of government
   b. nation-state
   c. improvement
   d. change in form or condition
4. When soldiers went to battle, they would wear heavy suits of armor. These suits protected them from spears and swords. However, they gave no protection against guns.
   Suits of **armor** are actually suits of
   a. spears
   b. metal
   c. heavy firearms
   d. battle
5. The modern nation-states were well organized and could wage wars using many more soldiers than before. Because more soldiers were fighting, wars became much bloodier.

Wage in this passage means

a. to pay for
b. to fight
c. to organize
d. to use

6. After the decline of feudalism, more soldiers became involved in wars, and armies became larger.

Involved probably means

a. taking part in
b. declining
c. becoming larger
d. ending

7. Gunpowder was important in bringing an end to feudalism. This substance, which helps make guns work, changed the way in which wars were being fought.

Gunpowder is

a. something new
b. firearms
c. something a soldier eats
d. something a soldier needs for his gun

8. Guns were used in place of spears and swords during the decline of feudalism. These firearms needed gunpowder to make them work.

Firearms are

a. soldiers
b. guns
c. spears
d. gunpowder

9. Swords and spears were examples of weapons used before the discovery of gunpowder. These instruments, which were used to fight wars, were soon replaced with more modern weapons called firearms.

Weapons are

a. examples
b. instruments used to fight wars
c. modern instruments
d. instruments used to replace swords

Exercise 16

Answer the following questions, based on the Reading Exercise passage.

1. When did the nation-state begin to take the place of the old system of small private states?

____

2. Why were these modern nation-states stronger?

____

3. What took the place of spears and swords?

____

4. What is a sword?

____

5. What could protect men against spears and swords?

____

6. What facilitated the transition from feudalism to the nation-state?

____

7. Who became more important as soldiers?

____

Lesson 2

The Development of Prison Systems

PREREADING ACTIVITIES

A. Discussion Questions

1. Have you ever visited a prison? What was it like?
2. Why are people sent to prison?
3. What is the purpose of a prison?
4. How can society benefit from prisons?

B. Special Vocabulary (Marked "*" in Passage A)

preliminary detention	a period of being kept within bounds while waiting trial
torture	the causing of severe pain as a means of punishment or of forcing one to do something against one's will

C. Guide Questions

As you read Passage A, ask yourself the following questions:

1. What have only recently been used to punish people for wrong acts?
2. A long time ago, why were people kept in prison?

3. Why did the people of Europe become angry near the end of the Middle Ages?
4. Who brought with them the idea of keeping every prisoner alone in a small room?
5. What jail in America worked on the idea of allowing prisoners to go after a long period of being alone?
6. Who stopped the system of keeping every prisoner alone in a small room?
7. Where was a new place built for young people who did something wrong?
8. What were the important ideas of this system?

NOW READ PASSAGE A. WHEN YOU FINISH READING, ANSWER THE GUIDE QUESTIONS.

READING PASSAGES

The Development of Prison Systems

Written by Edward Weidhmann, 1977

Passage A

In the history of the human race, prisons have only **recently** been used to **punish people** for **wrong acts.** A long time ago prisons were places of *preliminary detention only. People were kept in prison to wait for *torture, **death,** or other cruel punishment. **Near the end of** the Middle Ages[1] the people of Europe became angry about the **cruel acts** of that system and **disagreed strongly.** Therefore, less cruel techniques of punishment were used. For example, **people were sent away from their country and were never allowed to come back,** or they were **kept in prison.**

The early settlers of America[2] brought with them the idea of **keeping** every prisoner **alone** in a small room. The prisoners could not see or talk to each other and they could only read and exercise by themselves. After a long **period of being alone,** the prisoners could be **allowed to go** because they would not **do** any more wrong acts. The Walnut Street Jail in America **worked** on this idea. **At the end** of the eighteenth century, however, a religious group stopped that system.

About the time of the American Civil War,[3] a new **place** for young

[1]Middle Ages (476–1450) The period of European history between ancient and modern times.

[2]People first went to live in America in the early part of the seventeenth century.

[3]American Civil War (1861–1865) The war in the United States between the Northern states and the Southern states.

people who did something wrong was built in Elmira, New York. This new system worked on the **important ideas** of **putting** prisoners of the same age **into one group, educating** them, and training them.

At the end of the nineteenth century, a new idea was **started.** It **allowed** prisoners to work together during the day. It also **made** some problems of **controlling** the prison **fewer. Later** many prisons were built in America and **in the other countries** which worked on this idea.

NOW GO BACK AND ANSWER THE GUIDE QUESTIONS.

Passage B

In the history of the human race, the use of prisons as **punishment** for **crimes** is **of** fairly **recent origin.** A long time ago, prisons were merely places of preliminary detention. People were locked up in them to wait for torture, **execution,** or other cruel punishment. **In the late** Middle Ages the people of Europe became angry about the **cruelties** of that system and **protested.** Therefore, less cruel techniques of punishment were used, such as **banishment** and **imprisonment.**

The early settlers of America brought with them the idea of **isolating** prisoners. They could not see or talk to each other and could only read and exercise by themselves. After a long **isolation,** the prisoners could be **released** because they would not **commit** any more crimes. The Walnut Street Jail in America **operated** on this idea. **In the latter part** of the eighteenth century, however, a religious group stopped that system.

At the end of the nineteenth century, a new idea was **introduced.** It **permitted** prisoners to work together in groups during the day. It also **reduced** problems of **administration. Afterward** many prisons were built in America and **abroad** which operated on this idea.

About the time of the American Civil War, a new **institution** for young **offenders** was built in Elmira, New York. This new system worked on the **principles** of **classifying** prisoners on the basis of age, **giving** them an **education** and training them.

COMPREHENSION EXERCISES

Exercise 1

Reread Passage B and answer the following questions:

1. When were prisons merely places of preliminary detention?

____

2. When did the people of Europe protest about the cruel system of punishment?

____

3. According to the American settlers, when could a prisoner be released?

____

4. When was the system of isolation of prisoners stopped?

____

5. When were prisoners first permitted to work in groups?

____

6. When did prisoners do their group work?

____

7. When was a new institution for young offenders built in Elmira?

____

Exercise 2

Reread Passage B and answer the following questions:

1. In line 3, *them* refers to _______________.
2. In line 5, *that system* refers to _______________.
3. In line 9, *they* refers to _______________.
4. In line 12, *this idea* refers to _______________

   _______________.
5. In line 13, *that system* refers to _______________

   _______________.
6. In line 15, *it* refers to _______________.
7. In line 17, *this idea* refers to _______________.
8. In line 19, *this new system* refers to _______________

   _______________.

VOCABULARY EXERCISES

Exercise 3

Find the word in the list that has nearly the same meaning as the phrase in parentheses below. Then write that word in the blank.

administration	execution	principles
classified	institutions	protested
commit	isolating	reduced
crimes	offenders	released

1. (acts against the law) People sometimes commit ________________ by mistake.
2. (to make less) Prisoners' time in prison is often ________________ if they behave well.
3. (management, control) The ________________ of prisons is a very difficult task that requires many years of experience and study.
4. (a basic truth, law, or belief) One of the ________________ of modern prisons is helping prisoners to become better persons.
5. (arranged according to class or type) Prisoners are ________________ according to age, sex, height, and weight.
6. (people who break a moral or social law) ________________ are punished by imprisonment, fines, or public opinion.
7. (to do something) When people ________________ crimes, they hurt society.
8. (to set free) When you pay your parking ticket, your car will be ________________ from the police garage.
9. (to feel or express dislike for something) The prisoners ________________ against the bad food in prison.
10. (organizations that serve the public) ________________ were built that helped young offenders.
11. (punishment by death) Centuries ago ________________ was more common than imprisonment.
12. (to separate from a group or whole and set aside) ________________ prisoners was thought to be a way to make them better people.

Exercise 4

Choose the word from the list that best completes each of the sentences in the paragraph below and write it in the blank. Each word is used only once.

administration	execution	principles
classified	institutions	protested
commit	isolating	reduced
crimes	offenders	released

The use of prisons as a punishment for ________________ is of fairly recent origin. Long ago ________________ were locked up in them to wait for torture, ________________, or other cruel punishment. Later the idea of ________________ each prisoner was used. The prisoners could be ________________ only after a long isolation, in the belief that they would not ________________ any more wrong acts. A religious group ________________ against this idea. Now prisoners are permitted to work together in groups. They are ________________ on the basis of age, they are given an education, and they are trained. ________________ that work on these ________________ help prisoners as well as punish them. This system has also ________________ problems of ________________.

WORD SKILLS

A. The noun suffix *-ment*

Examples from Passage B: banish*ment* (l. 7)
imprison*ment* (l. 7)
punish*ment* (l. 1)

The suffix *-ment* is added to verbs to form nouns.

Examples:	*Verb*	*Noun*
	achieve	achievement
	govern	government

Exercise 5

Write the correct verb form for the underlined noun in each of the sentences below. Be sure to use the correct verb tense.

Example: They made an agreement to build a new water system.
They ____agreed____ to build a new water system.

1. She received lots of encouragement to attend the Olympic Games.

   She was ________________ very much to attend the Olympic Games.

2. It was a great <u>disappointment</u> for Sylvia not to be accepted by a university.

   Sylvia was greatly ______________________ that she was not accepted by a university.
3. He did not make any <u>improvement</u> in English last year.

   He did not ______________________ his English last year.
4. Their <u>measurement</u> of the company's growth was very thorough.

   They ______________________ the company's growth very thoroughly.
5. The country's <u>development</u> has moved very rapidly.

   The country has ______________________ very rapidly.

B. The suffix *-ward*

Example from Passage B: after*ward* (l. 16)

The suffix *-ward* is added to words to form adverbs or adjectives and usually means "in the direction of" or "toward."

Examples:	eastward	toward the east
	forward	toward the front; ahead

Exercise 6

Write the adverb ending in *-ward* for the underlined word or phrase in each sentence below.

1. The plane flew <u>in a southerly direction</u> for 200 miles.

   The plane flew ______________________ for 200 miles.
2. You go to the meeting and I'll see you <u>after it is over</u>.

   You go to the meeting and I'll see you ______________________.
3. After a brief stop, the bus traveled <u>on</u>, to the end of its route.

   After a brief stop, the bus traveled ______________________, to the end of its route.
4. Please move <u>toward the front</u>; dinner is going to be served now.

   Please move ______________________; dinner is going to be served now.

C. The noun suffixes *-er* and *-or*

Examples from Passage B: offend*er*s (l. 19)
prison*er*s (l. 9)

The suffixes -*er* and -*or* are agent noun suffixes. These suffixes are usually added to *verbs* to form *agent nouns*. They usually mean "a person who" or "a thing that."

Examples:	*Verb*	*Agent Noun*	*Meaning*
	erase	eraser	a thing that erases
	visit	visitor	a person who visits

The suffix -*er* is dometimes added to nouns or adjectives to form agent nouns.

Examples:		
	law	lawyer*
	London	Londoner
	prison	prisoner

*Note spelling change.

Exercise 7

Write the verb form or noun for the underlined agent noun in each of the sentences below. Be sure to put the verb in the correct tense.

Examples: The organizer of the project was Dr. Rivera.
Dr. Rivera ___organized___ the project.

Mr. Whitman is a hatter.
Mr. Whitman is a person who makes
___hats___.

1. Settlers first came to Jamestown, Virginia, in 1607.

   The first people who __________ in Jamestown came in 1607.
2. We hope to find a buyer for our house.

   We hope to find someone who will __________ our house.
3. This factory is a very large employer.

   This factory __________ many people.
4. She is an advisor to the president.

   She is a person who __________ the president.
5. National Panasonic and Sony are two major competitors in the television market.

   National Panasonic and Sony are two major companies that __________ for the television market.
6. Confucius was known as a philosopher.

   Confucius was known as a person who knew about __________.

7. Marsha Phillips is a lawyer for one of the large oil companies.

   Marsha Phillips is a person who practices ____________ for one of the large oil companies.

8. There are many foreigners in California.

   There are many people from ____________ countries in California.

9. Miss Abraham is a southerner.

   Miss Abraham is from the ____________ part of the country.

10. Londoners must be used to damp, foggy weather.

    People who live in ____________ must be used to damp, foggy weather.

DISCOURSE SKILLS

Exercise 8

Each of the phrases below refers to a time in Passage B. Number these *specific time periods* in the blanks, in the order in which they actually happened in history. Write "1" for the time period that happened first.

_______1. in the latter part of the eighteenth century

_______2. a long time ago, before the Middle Ages

_______3. about the time of the American Civil War

_______4. the early settlers of America

_______5. in the late Middle Ages

_______6. at the end of the nineteenth century

Exercise 9

Below is a time chart of the time periods that are mentioned in Passage B. In blank A write the general time of the whole passage. In blanks 1–6 write the specific time periods from Exercise 8. In the other blanks write the correct letters for the events or conditions that happened or existed in each period. These events and conditions are listed below the chart. If more than one event or condition happened in one time period, write them in the order in which they happened.

General Time of the Passage	Specific Time Periods	Events or Conditions
	6. ______________________	________
	5. ______________________	________
A. ______________	4. ______________________	________
______________	3. ______________________	________
______________	2. ______________________	________
	1. ______________________	________

Events and Conditions

A. Prisoners were classified according to age.
B. People protested against the cruel system of punishment.
C. People were banished from their country as punishment.
D. Other prisons were built that used group work.
E. Prisons were used for preliminary detention.
F. Group work with prisoners was introduced.
G. Prisons were first used as punishment for wrong acts.
H. The system of isolation was stopped.
I. Prisoners were isolated.
J. People were locked up to wait for punishment.
K. Prisoners were released after a long isolation.
L. Prisoners were given an education and training.

Exercise 10

Time phrases with *in, at, during, about,* and *on*

Look at the questions in Exercise 1. Write the numbers of the questions whose answers begin with the prepositions *in, at, during,* or *about.*

______ ______ ______ ______ ______

These phrases in Passage B are used to refer to the *time periods* when something happened:

in the late Middle Ages (l. 4)
in the latter part of the eighteenth century (l. 12)
at the end of the nineteenth century (l. 14)
during the day (l. 15)
about the time of the American Civil War (l. 18)

Phrases with the words *at* and *about* are used to refer to specific *points* in time.

Examples:	at 5 o'clock	about 5 o'clock
	at 6 A.M.	about 6 A.M.

Note: *At* means "exactly" at the time mentioned; *about* means "very nearly" the time mentioned.

Phrases with the words *in* or *during* are used to refer to specific *periods* of time.

Examples:	in the morning	during the morning
	in April	during April
	in the summer	during the summer
	in 1983	during 1983
	in the twelfth century	during the twelfth century
	in the following year	during the following year

***On* is used with days of the week and specific days or parts of days.**

Examples: on Tuesday
on Monday morning
on July 4
on the following day

Choose the time word (*in, at, on, during,* or *about*) that best completes each of the following sentences and write it in the blank. Each time word is used more than once.

1. A new place for young offenders was built ________________ the time of the American Civil War.
2. ________________ Tuesday night there is a meeting at the university.
3. We plan to take a trip to Europe ________________ the summer.
4. A new idea about prison administration was introduced ________________ the end of the nineteenth century.
5. Prisoners could work together in groups ________________ the day.
6. We have English class ________________ the morning and economics class ________________ the afternoon.
7. The library usually opens ________________ 8 o'clock ________________ the morning.

8. Students and teachers usually eat lunch ______________________ noon every day.

9. ______________________ the late Middle Ages the people of Europe protested against the cruelties of the system of punishment.

10. Prisoners were permitted to exercise only ______________________ certain days.

READING EXERCISE

Read the passage below and then do the exercises that follow.

When a person commits a crime, he is not always sent to prison. If he has committed some minor offense, he may be released from detention and allowed to remain in the community. This type of punishment is usually administered to juveniles. It is young people who usually commit the less serious crimes. For this reason they are given less punishment. Although the individual is not in jail, he is under the supervision of special police officers. These officers watch his actions very closely. This type of punishment is called probation.

The conditions of the probation are decided in a meeting during which a judge hears the offender's case. After this meeting, the judge issues an order of probation. This order can only be made with the offender's consent. If the offender does not wish to be placed on probation, he must go to jail.

Once on probation, the offender cannot disobey the probation order. He must report to the police at least once a week. During the whole period of probation, the offender must live according to the conditions ordered by the court. If there is a breach of the probation order, the offender may be taken off probation and placed in jail.

Written by Edward Weidhmann, 1977

Vocabulary in Context

In the passage above there were probably several words that you did not know. In Lesson 1, you learned that you can find the meaning of words from the *context* by asking certain questions. The example below shows you another method for finding the meaning of a word from its context.

"Minor" is an **adjective.** We know this because it comes before the **noun** "offense." "Minor" describes what kind of offense we are referring to. Sometimes we can understand the meaning of a word if we know that it refers to another word or phrase in the passage. In line 4 we read that young people "commit" less serious crimes. So "minor offenses" and "less serious crimes" are both **objects** of the **verb** "commit" and probably refer to the same thing. We also know that when someone commits a "minor offense," the punishment will be less. People who commit "less serious crimes" are also given "less punishment." Thus we can be sure that the phrases "minor offenses" and "less serious crimes" refer to the same thing and are probably similar in meaning. Thus "minor," the adjective that describes "offenses," means the same as "less serious," which describes "crimes." We can see that "offenses" and "crimes" are similar in meaning as well.

Using this method, do the following exercises.

Exercise 11

In each blank below, write the word from the passage that has nearly the same meaning as the **boldface** word or phrase.

1. The term of probation was determined in **a legal meeting during which a judge heard the offender's case.**

   ____

2. Since the offender committed a **less serious** offense, he was put on probation by the court.

   ____

3. Although her **crime** was a small one, she was given a three-year sentence.

   ____

4. Probation is the punishment often **given** to people who commit a minor offense.

   ____

5. **Young people** who commit crimes are not always sent to prison.

   ____

6. The offender was kept under **close watch** by the officers.

   ____

7. The offender was **allowed to stay in the community** and he was **watched carefully by probation officers.**

   ____

8. The court knew that the offender would **agree** to the decision to put him on probation.

   ____

9. If you **disobey** the probation order, you may have to go to prison.

   ____

10. The offender may have to go to **prison** if he breaches the probation order.

   ____

Exercise 12

Read the following short passages and select the best answer from the choices given for each. Circle the letter for the word you choose.

1. The young person committed only a minor offense. Since the crime was small and not very serious, the court decided to put the offender on probation.

   In this passage, **minor** means

   a. large and important
   b. committed
   c. small and not very serious
   d. serious

2. To decide whether to place the offender on probation, he was taken to a legal meeting. Since the crime was very serious, the court decided to place the offender in jail.

   In this passage, **court** means

   a. an order
   b. a large building
   c. a legal meeting
   d. a prison

3. The man committed many offenses in less than a year. Since so many crimes were committed, the court would not give him probation.

   The word **offenses** means

   a. probations
   b. courts
   c. crimes
   d. serious

4. The courts usually administer less punishment to young offenders. Sometimes the parents of these offenders give more punishment to their children when they come home.

   Administer means

   a. give
   b. punish
   c. courts
   d. offense

5. Under the law, juveniles are not punished in the same way that adults are punished. Usually young people are put on probation. Adults may be sent to jail for the same offense.

   Juveniles refers to

   a. adults
   b. young people
   c. serious
   d. punishment

6. Individuals on probation are under the supervision of police or probation officers. The offenders are watched closely so that they do not commit another offense. If they do, they may have to return to jail.

   Supervision means

   a. probation
   b. offense
   c. close, careful watch
   d. return

7. Courts sometimes put offenders on probation if their crimes are not serious. They are allowed to remain in the community, but are watched very closely.

Probation means the offender

a. is put in jail
b. is watched closely
c. is not serious
d. remains in the community and is watched closely

8. If the offender gives his consent to the order, he will be put on probation. If he does not agree to the order, he may be sent to jail.

To **consent** means

a. to order
b. to give
c. to agree
d. to go to jail

9. If there is a breach of the probation order, the offender is no longer allowed on probation. Since he disobeyed the probation order, he may be sent to jail.

Breach means

a. to go to jail
b. to disobey
c. to offend
d. to consent

10. In prison there is little excitement and less freedom. For this reason, if the offender can, he will usually choose probation instead of jail.

Jail means

a. choice
b. reason
c. excitement
d. prison

Exercise 13

Answer the following questions, based on the Reading Exercise passage.

1. Where are offenders on probation allowed to remain?

____

2. Why are juveniles usually placed on probation?

____

3. How often must an offender on probation report to the police?

____

4. Who orders the conditions of the probation?

____

5. Where must an offender go if he or she does not wish to be placed on probation?

____

6. What happens if the offender breaches the probation order?

____

Lesson 3

The Selection and Training of Police Officers

PREREADING ACTIVITIES

A. Discussion Questions

1. Have you ever wanted to be a police officer? Why or why not?
2. How difficult do you think a police officer's job is?
3. What skills and knowledge do police officers need for their job?
4. Do you think anyone could become a police officer? Why or why not?

B. Special Vocabulary (Marked "*" in Passage A)

candidate	a person who seeks an office or a position
probationary	for a trial period
constable	a police officer
first aid	emergency treatment administered before professional medical care is available
force	a group of persons organized for a particular purpose
division	a territory organized as a unit for administrative purposes
probation	a trial period
sergeant	a rank of police officer

C. Guide Questions

As you read Passage A, ask yourself the following questions:

1. What does this reading describe?
2. Where does the candidate have to answer several questions?
3. When is the candidate given an examination of the body?
4. How long does a probationary constable stay at the police training center?
5. When does the probationary constable receive teaching in police skills?
6. Does the student officer finish his training at the police training center?
7. Where does the student officer go after he leaves the police training center?
8. What does the officer study at the police division?
9. During the two-year training period, where does the probationary constable go twice for more courses?
10. What two things must happen before the constable can be made a sergeant?

NOW READ PASSAGE A. WHEN YOU FINISH READING, ANSWER THE GUIDE QUESTIONS.

READING PASSAGES

The Selection and Training of Police Officers

Adapted from James Cramer, 1968

Passage A

This **reading** describes the **way** police officers in England and Wales **are chosen** and **taught.** First the candidate is invited to a **meeting** where he has **to answer several questions.** Then the examining persons find out about his health by giving him a complete **examination of the body.** After these steps are successfully completed, the candidate is accepted as a *probationary *constable. He is then sent to a police training center, where he lives for 13 weeks. During that time, he receives **teaching** in various police skills. This teaching includes everyday police duties, **the way to discover** and **stop** crime, basic courses in law, and other kinds of police work. He is taught **how to keep in good physical condition** and is given useful exercises. In addition to these, he is also taught how to provide *first aid and help in saving lives.

After this course, the **student officer** returns to his own police *force, where he is given more information about different police skills. He then joins a police *division and receives practical training in the writing of reports and other skills which are **necessary** for a police officer. During the two years' *probation, the candidate's progress is **watched** by his superior officers. They write reports about whether he has been **well chosen for the job** and **give** them **to** the organizers of the training program. They also write about the **quality** of his work as a police officer. During the two-year period, the probationary constable returns twice to the training center for courses of **medium-** and **higher-level difficulty.** Each of these return training courses is two weeks **long.**

Before the constable **is suitable** for **a higher position** and can be made a *sergeant, he must pass examinations. These examinations are in educational subjects, police duties, criminal law, the **organization** of the central and town government, and so on. He must also have completed five years' service.

NOW GO BACK AND ANSWER THE GUIDE QUESTIONS.

Passage B

This **article** describes the **procedure** for the **selection** and **training** of police officers in England and Wales. After the candidate passes an **interview** and a complete **physical checkup,** he is accepted as a probationary constable. He is then sent to a police training center, where he lives for 13 weeks. During that time he receives a course of **instruction** in everyday police duties, **detection** and **prevention** of crime, basic courses in law, and other kinds of police work. Instruction in **physical training** and exercise, first aid, and life saving is also given.

After this course, the **trainee** returns to his own police force for more instruction. He then joins a police division and receives practical training in report writing and other skills **essential** to a police officer. His progress is **noted** by his superior officers. While training him, they **submit** reports on his **suitability** and **standard** of work for the period of his two years' probation. During the two-year period, the probationary constable returns twice to the training center for **intermediate** and **advanced** courses, each of two weeks' **duration.**

To **qualify** for **promotion** to sergeant, a constable must pass examinations in educational subjects, police duties, criminal law, the **structure** of central and local government, and so on. He must also have completed five years' service.

COMPREHENSION EXERCISES

Exercise 1

Reread Passage B, and then answer the following questions.

1. In line 3, *he* refers to ______.
2. In line 4, *He* refers to ______.
3. In line 5, *that time* refers to ______.
4. In line 9, *this course* refers to ______.
5. In line 10, *He* refers to ______.
6. In line 12, *they* refers to ______.
7. In line 19, *He* refers to ______.
8. In lines 7–8, some information is left out of the sentence (this is often the case in passive sentences). To whom is the instruction given?

   ______

Exercise 2

In Exercise 1, the word *he* refers to several different words or phrases. Write these words and phrases below.

1. ______ (l. 3)
2. ______ (l. 4)
3. ______ (l. 10)
4. ______ (l. 19)

These words or phrases refer to the same person as he goes through the different steps in a procedure. What procedure is it?

5. ______

Exercise 3

In Passage B several different words or phrases are used to refer to *a person who does police work.* Write these words or phrases below.

1. ______ (l. 2)
2. ______ (l. 3)
3. ______ (l. 11)
4. ______ (l. 17)

Several different words are also used to refer to the *teaching* that the person receives. Write these words below.

5. ______ (l. 1)

6. ______________________ (l. 5)
7. ______________________ (l. 7)

In Exercises 2 and 3, you saw that a writer often repeats a word or uses words with similar meaning in order to show the connection between different parts of a passage. For example, in line 4 the phrase *probationary constable* is used.

In lines 17–18 the writer says

8. a ______________________ must pass examinations

By using words with similar meaning, the writer helps the reader understand the connection between these two paragraphs and that the writer's explanation of the process of becoming a police officer is continued in the third paragraph.

VOCABULARY EXERCISES

Exercise 4

Find the word in the list that each phrase in parentheses best defines. Write that word in the blank to complete the sentence.

detection	interview	qualify
essential	physical	structure
instruction	procedure	submit
intermediate	promotion	

1. (able to do the work needed by a job or position) These persons ______________________ for the position of sergeant.
2. (a meeting where questions are asked) If you want to become a police officer, you must begin by attending an ______________________.
3. (a higher position or rank) The constable passed the examination. Now he will receive a ______________________ to sergeant.
4. (lessons; education; teaching) The ______________________ that the probationary constables receive helps them to become good police officers.
5. (medium level; in the middle) The candidates must study beginning, ______________________, and advanced courses in law.
6. (a series of steps; a course of action) The ______________________ for

becoming a police officer begins with an interview and a physical checkup.

7. (of the greatest importance) Being able to prevent and detect crime is an ____________ part of the police officer's work.
8. (organization; arrangement) The candidate must understand the ____________ of local and central government.
9. (discovery or finding out) The prevention and ____________ of crime is one of the subjects a candidate must study.
10. (of the body) Frequent ____________ checkups are necessary for good health.
11. (to give something to somebody else for consideration) The superior officers of the candidates must ____________ reports about them.

Exercise 5

Fill in the blanks with words from the list. Each word is used only once.

detection	interview	qualify
essential	physical	structure
instruction	procedure	submit
intermediate	promotion	

The article describes the ____________ for choosing and training police officers. The candidate must first attend an ____________ and have a complete ____________ checkup. If the candidate is accepted, he then goes to live at a police training center where he receives ____________ in crime prevention and ____________. He also studies other ____________ beginning and ____________ subjects, such as law, the ____________ of local and central government, and police duties. During his two years as a probationary constable, he is watched carefully by his superior officers, and they ____________ reports about him. Later, after he has completed five years' service, to ____________ for ____________ to sergeant, a constable must pass an examination.

WORD SKILLS

A. The adjective suffixes *-able* and *-ible*

Example from Passage A: suit*able* (l. 23)

The suffixes *-able* and *-ible* are usually added to verbs to form adjectives. They usually mean "able to."

Examples:	*Verb*	*Adjective*	*Meaning*
	agree	agreeable	able to agree
	divide	divisible*	able to be divided

The suffixes *-able* and *-ible* are sometimes added to nouns to form adjectives.

Examples: *Noun*	*Adjective*
desire	desirable*
honor	honorable

*Note spelling change.

Exercise 6

Fill in each blank below with one of the following words:

observable	reasonable	suitable
possible	responsible	

1. I believe that it is not ____________________ to solve that problem; it is too difficult.
2. Who is ____________________ for the electrical problems we have been having?
3. This office will be quite ____________________ for our needs. It's exactly the right size for a law office.
4. It is ____________________ to assume that the housing problem will be solved within the next five years.
5. The professor's actions were not ____________________ because she was hidden from our view by the blackboard.

B. The noun suffix *-ity*

Example from Passage B: suitabil*ity* (l. 13)

The suffix *-ity* is usually added to adjectives to form nouns. It is most frequently added to adjectives ending with *-able* and *-ible*.

Examples: *Adjective*	*Noun*
operable	operability*
probable	probability*

The suffix *-ity* is also added to adjectives ending in *-al*.

Examples: *Adjective*	*Noun*
national	nationality
practical	practicality

The suffix *-ity* is sometimes added to nouns.

Examples: *Noun*	*Noun*
acid	acidity
fluid	fluidity

*Note spelling change from *-bl-* to *-bil-*.

Exercise 7

Answer the following questions using the noun form for the underlined words.

1. Do you think it is <u>probable</u> that the price of food will go down?

   No, I think the ______________________ of that happening is zero.
2. Did you buy that car because it was <u>dependable</u>?

   Yes, it's famous for its ______________________.
3. Is that plan really <u>practical</u>?

   No, I think its ______________________ is questionable.
4. Does she have <u>suitable</u> training and character to become a police officer?

   Her training is excellent, but the ______________________ of her character worries me.
5. Are the products of these two factories <u>similar</u>?

   Yes, the ______________________ of their products is beyond a doubt.

Exercise 8

Fill in the following chart with the correct word forms:

Stem	*Adjective* (-ible, -able, -al)	*Noun* (-ity)
1. ____________	________________	describability
2. ____________	sensible	________________
3. ____________	________________	personality
4. ____________	________________	responsibility
5. respect	________________	________________

C. The noun suffix *-ee*

Example from Passage B: train*ee* (l. 9)

The suffix -ee is usually added to verbs to form nouns. It usually means "the receiver of an action" or "a person in a certain condition."

Examples:	*Verb*	*Noun*	*Meaning*
	absent	absentee	a person who is absent
	appoint	appointee	a person who is appointed to a position
	employ	employee	a person who is employed

Nouns ending in -ee often have corresponding agent nouns ending in *-er* or *-or*.

Examples:	*-ee Noun*	*Agent Noun*
	employee	employer
	examinee	examiner
	trainee	trainer

Exercise 9

Fill in the blanks in the following sentences with the correct verb forms, the *-ee* nouns, and the *-er* or *-or* agent nouns.

1. employ — Geraldine and Sarah Smith are both ________________ by the Xerox Company.
   The Xerox Company is the ________________.
   Geraldine and Sarah Smith are two of the ________________.

2. pay — Ali must ________________ the money to Mr. Brown today.
   Ali is the ________________.
   Mr. Brown is the ________________.

3. examine The professor will ______________ the students tomorrow.
   The professor is the ______________.
   The students are the ______________.
4. grant The university ______________ $1,000,000 to the hospital for new medical equipment.
   The university is the ______________.
   The hospital is the ______________.
5. address Ms. Alvarez ______________ her letter to the First National Bank.
   Ms. Alvarez is the ______________.
   The First National Bank is the ______________.

D. The verb suffix *-ify*

Example from Passage B: qual*ify* (l. 17)

The suffix *-ify* is added to stems to form verbs. It usually means "making," "giving," "having," or "becoming."

Examples: *Stem*	*Verb*
electric	electrify*
example	exemplify*

*Note spelling change.

Exercise 10

Write the correct *-ify* verb form for the underlined words in each sentence below. Choose your answers from the words in the following list:

certify notify simplify
classify qualify

1. She made certain that the check was acceptable by calling the bank.

   She ______________ the acceptability of the check by calling the bank.
2. He gave notice to the employees that the office would be closed tomorrow.

   He ______________ the employees that the office would be closed tomorrow.
3. The teacher made the lesson simple by having each student do the experiment.

   The teacher ______________ the lesson by having each student do the experiment.

4. The professor grouped the people of the city into three classes—lower class, middle class, and upper class.

   The professor ______________________ the people of the city into lower, middle, and upper classes.

5. Does he have the qualities needed for the job?

   Does he ______________________ for the job?

DISCOURSE SKILLS

Exercise 11

Reread the first paragraph in Passage B. Every event in this paragraph is a *step* in the procedure of selecting and training police officers. Below is a list of these steps. They are not in the correct order. Fill in each blank with the correct verb from the list below:

accepted	interviewed	receives
given	lives	sent

A. The candidate is ______________________ as a probationary constable.

B. The candidate is ______________________ before being physically examined.

C. The candidate is ______________________ to a police training center.

D. The candidate is ______________________ a physical checkup after being accepted at the interview.

E. The candidate ______________________ instruction in various subjects at the police training center.

F. The candidate ______________________ at the police training center for 13 weeks.

Exercise 12

The steps in Exercise 11 were not given in their correct order. In the blanks below, write the letters of the steps in the order in which they appear in the first paragraph of Passage B.

1. ______________________ 4. ______________________

2. ______________________ 5. ______________________

3. ______________________ 6. ______________________

Two of these steps or events happen during the same time period.

Events that happen *at the same time* are *simultaneous.*

What two events in paragraph 1 are simultaneous?

7. ______________________________

8. ______________________________

What time phrase shows that these events are simultaneous?

9. ______________________________

Exercise 13

The second paragraph in Passage B describes what happens after the first 13 weeks. Below is a list of the events in the second paragraph. They are not in the correct order. Fill in the blanks with the correct word or phrase.

A. The trainee's progress is ______________ by his superior officers.

B. The trainee ______________ a police division.

C. The trainee ______________ to his own police force.

D. Officers ______________ reports on the trainee's suitability and standard of work.

E. The trainee ______________ practical training in various subjects.

F. The trainee ______________ twice to the police training center.

Exercise 14

The events in Exercise 13 were not given in their correct order. In the blanks below, write the letters of the events as they appear in the second paragraph of Passage B.

1. ______________ 4. ______________

2. ______________ 5. ______________

3. ______________ 6. ______________

Exercise 15

Events that happen during the same time period, or at the same time, are *simultaneous* events.

Four of the events in the second paragraph of Passage B happen within the same time period; they are simultaneous. In the blanks below, write the events that happen during the same time period. These events are listed in Exercise 13.

During this period

1. ______________________________

2. ______________________________

3. ______________________________

4. ______________________________

Where did these four simultaneous events happen?

5. at a ______________________________

During what time period did these four simultaneous events happen?

6. ______________________________

READING EXERCISE

Read the passage below and then do the exercises that follow.

The basic training given in city police forces usually includes a 10- to 20-week police skills program at the initial stage of the new police officer's service. These first steps in the police skills program are followed by field experience with little or no further training. In this on-the-job experience, formal classroom learning is kept apart from practical police experience.

Some people believe that there is a better method than keeping the two teaching methods separate. They believe that instead of separate instruction, police skill training and formal education should be offered together. This program would also include human relations and guided practical field experience. In addition, certain courses would be given credit by universities. This would encourage the police officers to continue their education after their basic training has been completed. With programs such as these, police officers would no longer avoid the idea of returning to the university. Instead of staying away from classroom study, they would have an incentive to continue. University credit gives the officers a good reward. It would give them something to work for.

Adapted from James Cramer, 1968

Vocabulary in Context

In the passage above there were probably several words that you did not know. The example below shows you how you can discover the meaning of one of these words.

"Avoid" is a **verb.** We know this because of its position in the sentence. "Avoid" is what the "police officers" do to the "idea of returning to the university." Our next step is to see if we can find another verb in the other sentences in the passage that means the same thing. In the sentence following the sentence with "avoid" we find a *synonym* for "returning to the university." This synonym, which means nearly the same thing as "returning to the university," is "classroom study." The verb used with "classroom study" is "staying away from." If "returning to the university" and "classroom study" mean almost the same thing, then we can be sure that "avoid" and "keeping away from" also have similar meanings.

Now do the following exercises.

Exercise 16

In each blank below, write the word from the Reading Exercise passage that has nearly the same meaning as the **boldface** word or phrase.

1. During the **first** period of their service, police officers are given a 10- to 20-week police skills program.

   ____

2. New police officers are given basic training during their first **period** of service.

   ____

3. During the police officer's **on-the-job** experience, formal classroom learning is kept apart from practical police experience.

   ____

4. Police skill training and formal education are **not** offered **together.**

   ____

5. Sometimes money is **what makes** many of **us want** to work.

   ____

6. Before being offered university credit, police officers would **keep away from** further university study.

   ____

Exercise 17

Read the following short passages and select the best answer from the choices given. Circle the letter for the best answer.

1. The initial stage of the program includes a 10- to 20-week police skills program. This initial stage is followed by field experience.
   Initial means
   a. first
   b. stages
   c. include
   d. skills
2. The initial stage includes a police skills program for new police officers. This is an important part of every police officer's basic training.
   Stage means
   a. basic
   b. initial
   c. training
   d. period
3. The police officer's initial training is followed by field experience. In this on-the-job experience, formal classroom learning is kept apart from practical police experience.
   Field means
   a. experience
   b. formal
   c. on-the-job
   d. initial
4. Formal classroom learning is separate from practical police experience. Some people believe that these two should not be kept apart. They believe that instead of separate instruction, police skill training and formal education should be offered together.
   Separate means
   a. method
   b. together
   c. experience
   d. kept apart; not together
5. When universities do not offer credit to police officers, they avoid the idea of returning to classes. If the universities started giving credit for classes, the officers would no longer stay away from the classroom.
   Avoid means
   a. to change
   b. to stay away from
   c. to enjoy
   d. to encourage
6. People always need an incentive to work. Some people work because they enjoy their jobs. Others work because they make a lot of money. Others want to gain more knowledge or meet new people. Still others work simply for the good of other people. All of these things are examples of what makes people want to work.
   Incentive means something that
   a. makes money
   b. makes you tired
   c. makes you want to do something
   d. helps you gain knowledge

Exercise 18

Answer the following questions, based on the Reading Exercise passage.

1. How long is the basic training in city police forces?

   ____

2. What follows the police skills program?

   ____

3. What might be a better method than the usual training method?

   ____

4. What would give police officers incentive to continue their education?

   ____

5. What two *new* ideas for training city police forces are discussed in the passage?

   ____

   ____

Lesson 4

Mr. Wilson's Bottling Business

PREREADING ACTIVITIES

A. Discussion Questions

1. Where are nationwide drinks, such as "Pepsi" and "7-Up," actually made?
2. How do nationwide companies make sure that their product is made with the same quality all over the United States?
3. What are the advantages for a local company to manufacture a nationwide product?
4. What are the disadvantages?

B. Special Vocabulary (Marked "*" in Passage A)

bankrupt	financially ruined; judged by a court of law as being unable to pay one's debts
Cheer-Up	the brand name of a particular drink
franchise	a right or authorization given by a manufacturer to a distributor or dealer
exclusive right	an authorization or permission given to one individual or company and to no others
syrup	a thick sweet liquid; a liquid produced by the main company and sold to local bottling companies for use in manufacturing a drink

C. Guide Questions

As you read Passage A, ask yourself the following questions:

1. What did Mr. Wilson do after he started his bottling business?
2. What were the two types of franchises for bottling "Cheer-Up"?
3. What did the franchises provide?
4. How often did the company have to renew the nonpermanent franchises?
5. To which factories were the nonpermanent franchises given?
6. Who owned the permanent franchises?
7. Why did Mr. Wilson's factory stop selling "Cheer-Up" during World War I?
8. When did Mr. Wilson start bottling "Cheer-Up" again?
9. Did Mr. Wilson ever obtain a permanent franchise?

NOW READ PASSAGE A. WHEN YOU FINISH READING, ANSWER THE GUIDE QUESTIONS.

READING PASSAGES

Mr. Wilson's Bottling Business

Adapted from Jack P. Wentworth, 1962

Passage A

George Wilson **found out** that a small **factory** for **putting drinks in bottles had become*** bankrupt. He bought its equipment and **started** a bottling business. **A short time after** he had started the business, Mr. Wilson **carefully examined** the possibility of bottling a drink called *"Cheer-Up." He found that *franchises were provided through a **particular method.**

The franchises, which provided the *exclusive right to bottle and sell "Cheer-Up," were **given** to bottling factories. Two types of franchises were given. Some were continued, or permanent, but others were **nonpermanent** and lasted **for only a limited time.** At that time, bottling factories which were **acceptable** could get nonpermanent franchises **without paying any money.** Each factory had to renew the franchise every two years. A permanent franchise was given after the factory had provided **suitable** equipment and when the "Cheer-Up" Company officials had **made sure** that the relationship between the company and the bottling factory was acceptable. Then the bottling company became the owner of the permanent franchise and could sell it. During the **following** years these franchises became very valuable.

Mr. Wilson's bottling factory received its nonpermanent franchise in 1916, but "Cheer-Up" was produced for only a short time before the United States entered World War I.[1] During the war, the price of sugar **increased,** with a **similar** increase in the price of "Cheer-Up" *syrup. Because of this, the company **stopped** bottling this **drink** until **after the war.** When the company **started** bottling **again,** the business increased, and Mr. Wilson was later able to obtain a permanent franchise.

NOW GO BACK AND ANSWER THE GUIDE QUESTIONS.

Passage B

When George Wilson **learned** that a small **bottling plant had gone** bankrupt, he bought its equipment and **established** a bottling business. **Shortly after** starting the business, Mr. Wilson **investigated** the bottling of "Cheer-Up." He found that the franchises were provided through a **certain process.**

The franchises, which provided the exclusive right to bottle and sell "Cheer-Up," were **issued** to bottling factories. Franchises of two types—permanent and **temporary**—were given. At that time, the temporary franchises were given **free** to anyone whom the "Cheer-Up" Company felt would make **satisfactory** bottlers. These temporary franchises had to be renewed every two years. A permanent franchise was issued after the **proper** equipment had been provided and when the "Cheer-Up" Company had **assured** that the relationship with the bottler was in every way satisfactory. This permanent franchise then became the property of the bottling company, and could be sold. During **subsequent** years, these franchises became very valuable.

The Wilson bottling plant received its temporary franchise in 1916, but "Cheer-Up" was bottled only for a short time before the United States entered World War I in 1917. At that time the price of sugar **advanced** so much, with a **corresponding** increase in the price of "Cheer-Up" syrup, that the company **discontinued** bottling this **beverage** until the **postwar** years. When bottling was **resumed,** the business increased and Mr. Wilson was later able to obtain a permanent franchise.

COMPREHENSION EXERCISES

Exercise 1

Reread Passage B, and then answer the following questions.

[1]World War I (1914–1918) A war in which Great Britain, France, Russia, the United States, and other allies fought against Germany, Austria-Hungary, Turkey, and Bulgaria.

1. When did George Wilson buy equipment and establish a bottling business?

   ____

2. When did Mr. Wilson investigate the bottling of "Cheer-Up?"

   ____

3. When were permanent franchises issued?

   ____

   and

   ____

4. When did the Wilson bottling plant receive its temporary franchise?

   ____

5. When did Mr. Wilson's plant discontinue bottling "Cheer-Up?"

   ____

6. When was bottling resumed?

   ____

7. The time expression *at that time* (l. 8) refers to the time when

   ____

8. The time expression *at that time* (l. 18) refers to the time when

   ____

Exercise 2

Reread Passage B and then number the events in each pair below, in the order in which they actually happened. Write "1" for the first event and "2" for the second.

______ 1. George Wilson bought equipment and established a bottling business.

______ George Wilson learned that a small bottling plant had gone bankrupt.

______ 2. Mr. Wilson started a business.

______ Mr. Wilson investigated the bottling of "Cheer-Up."

______ 3. Permanent franchises were issued.

______ The proper equipment had been provided and the "Cheer-Up" Company felt that the relationship with the bottler was in every way satisfactory.

_______ 4. The United States entered World War I.

_______ "Cheer-Up" was bottled for a short time.

Exercise 3

In Exercises 2 and 3 of Lesson 3, you learned that a writer often uses words with similar meanings to show the connection between different parts of a passage or to avoid repeating the same word many times. In Passage B there are several words that have similar meanings. Find these words and fill in the blanks below.

1. A small bottling ______________________ had gone bankrupt.
2. Franchises were issued to bottling ______________________.
3. In this passage ______________________ and ______________________ have nearly the same meaning: "a place or building where things are made."
4. George Wilson established a bottling ______________________.
5. The permanent franchises became the property of the bottling ______________________.
6. In this passage ______________________ and ______________________ have nearly the same meaning: "a type of organization."

VOCABULARY EXERCISES

Exercise 4

Read the definitions in parentheses below and then select the word that best completes each sentence. Choose the words from the list below.

certain	plant	satisfactory
corresponding	process	subsequent
investigated	proper	temporary
issued	resumed	

1. (examine carefully) Mr. Wilson ______________________ the idea of starting a bottling factory.
2. (factory) A small bottling ______________________ had gone bankrupt.

3. (something you do that causes a particular result) By following the ________________________ required by the "Cheer-Up" Company, Mr. Wilson could get a franchise.
4. (definite; established; fixed) A franchise was issued according to a ________________________ procedure.
5. (given out) Two kinds of franchises were ________________________.
6. (for a limited time) One kind of franchise was permanent and the other was ________________________.
7. (acceptable) The relations between Mr. Wilson and the "Cheer-Up" Company had to be ________________________.
8. (suitable) Mr. Wilson had to provide ________________________ bottling equipment.
9. (following in time or order) Franchises for bottling soft drinks frequently became very valuable in ________________________ years.
10. (similar or equivalent to something else) The price of sugar increased and there was a ________________________ increase in the price of syrup.
11. (began again) Mr. Wilson ________________________ the bottling of "Cheer-Up" after World War I.

Exercise 5

Fill in each blank with a word from the list below. Each word is used at least once.

certain	plant	satisfactory
corresponding	process	subsequent
investigated	proper	temporary
issued	resumed	

George Wilson ________________________ the possibility of bottling a soft drink called "Cheer-Up." He learned that a franchise would be ________________________ if a certain ________________________ was followed. The francise gave him the exclusive right to bottle and sell "Cheer-Up." The franchise ________________________ to him was ________________________ and had to be renewed every two years. If Mr. Wilson showed the "Cheer-Up" Company that he could provide ________________________ equipment and service, and if his relations with the company were ______________________,

he would be ______________________ a permanent franchise. The Wilson

bottling ______________________ received a ______________________

franchise in 1916. However, in the ______________________ years, because

of World War I, the price of sugar increased, with a ______________________ increase in the price of "Cheer-Up" syrup. The Wilson bottling

______________________ discontinued the bottling of this drink during

the war. Later it ______________________ the bottling of "Cheer-Up," and Mr. Wilson was able to obtain a permanent franchise.

WORD SKILLS

A. The noun suffix *-ness*

Example from Passage B: busi*ness* (l. 3)

The suffix *-ness* is usually added to adjectives to form nouns. It usually means a "state" or "quality."

Examples:	*Adjective*	*Noun*	*Meaning*
	busy	business*	a person's work or trade
	reasonable	reasonableness	the quality of being reasonable
	sad	sadness	the quality of being sad

The suffix *-ness* is often added to words ending in *-ly*.

Examples:	*-ly Words*	*Nouns*
	cleanly	cleanliness*
	friendly	friendliness*
	lonely	loneliness*

*Note spelling change.

Exercise 6

Fill in each blank below with the correct noun formed by adding *-ness* to an adjective in the list.

careless	great	lonely
friendly	lively	

1. The careless student made a lot of mistakes in his homework. The teacher was disappointed with his ____________.
2. Winston Churchill was a great leader of the British government during World War II. His ____________ is recognized by all students of history.
3. That young man is very friendly and is liked because of this. But his laziness sometimes makes people forget his ____________.
4. Hiroko had no friends and was very lonely. The ____________ that she felt was so great that she decided to return to her own country.
5. The young children playing in the park were very lively. Their ____________ made the old woman smile.

B. The suffix *-ship*

Example from Passage B: relation*ship* (ll. 12–13)

The suffix *-ship* is a noun suffix. It is usually added to other nouns. It can mean a "state," "condition," "quality," "office," or "ability."

Examples:	*Noun*	*Noun*	*Meaning*
	friend	friendship	the condition of being friends with someone
	governor	governorship	the office of being governor
	leader	leadership	the ability to be a leader

Exercise 7

Fill in the blanks with the correct *-ship* nouns, using the words from the list below.

hard	leader	sportsman
governor	relation	

1. What is the ____________ between height and weight?
2. Because of the president's excellent ____________, the country's condition is much better than before.
3. Carmen showed good ____________ by shaking hands with her opponent after the game.

4. If she is elected to the ______________________, I think the people of the state will have a very good leader.
5. When the economy of a country fails, life becomes difficult, and people experience a great deal of ______________________.

C. The prefix *post-*

Example from Passage B: *post*war (l. 20)

***Post-* is a prefix meaning "after in time," "later than," or "following."**

Examples:	*Word*	*Meaning*
	postgraduate	after graduation
	postoperative	after an operation
	postwar	after a war

Exercise 8

Fill in each blank below with the word from the list that best completes the sentence.

postdate	postoperative	postwar
postgraduate	postpone	

1. During the period after the war, a lot of rebuilding had to be done.

   During the ______________________ period, a lot of rebuilding had to be done.
2. The period after an operation is almost as important as the operation itself.

   The ______________________ period is almost as important as the operation itself.
3. Let's put off our meeting until next week.

   Let's ______________________ our meeting until next week.
4. Ms. Chen will take a course of study after graduation.

   Ms. Chen will take a ______________________ course of study.
5. You may write next month's date on this check.

   You may ______________________ this check a month.

DISCOURSE SKILLS

Exercise 9

Reread the first paragraph in Passage B. This paragraph describes specific events that happened once, during a particular time period in the past. There are two time expressions that tell us the sequence of the events in this paragraph. What are they?

1. ______________________ George Wilson learned that . . .
2. ______________________ starting business, Mr. Wilson . . .

In the blanks below, number the events in the order in which they happened. Write "1" for the first event.

______ 3. George Wilson investigated.

______ 4. He bought the equipment.

______ 5. He found that the franchises were provided.

______ 6. He established a bottling business.

______ 7. George Wilson learned about something.

______ 8. A small bottling business went bankrupt.

Exercise 10

Reread the second paragraph in Passage B. This paragraph describes the steps in a process that happened repeatedly during a particular period of time.

1. What process is described in this paragraph?

   issuing ______________________
2. What time expression tells us the time period of this process?

   ______________________ the temporary franchises were given free
3. This time expression means "when ______________________."

Listed below are the steps in the process of issuing permanent franchises. Number these steps in the order in which they actually occurred. Write "1" for the first step.

______ 4. Permanent franchises were provided.

______ 5. The "Cheer-Up" Company felt that the relationship with the bottler was satisfactory.

_______ 6. Permanent franchises became very valuable.

_______ 7. Proper equipment was provided.

_______ 8. Permanent franchises became the property of the bottling company.

Exercise 11

Reread the third paragraph in Passage B. This paragraph describes specific events that happened once, during a particular time period in the past.

1. What is the beginning of the time period in this paragraph?

   ____

2. What time expression tells us when the price of sugar advanced?

   ____

3. This time expression means "when ____________________."

In the blanks below, number the events in the order in which they actually happened. Write "1" for the first event. Write the same number for events that were simultaneous.

_______ 4. The price of sugar advanced.

_______ 5. "Cheer-Up" was bottled for only a short time.

_______ 6. The bottling plant received its temporary franchise.

_______ 7. The United States entered World War I.

_______ 8. Business increased.

_______ 9. Mr. Wilson obtained a permanent franchise.

_______ 10. The company discontinued bottling.

_______ 11. The price of "Cheer-Up" syrup increased.

_______ 12. The company resumed bottling.

READING EXERCISE

Read the passage below and then do the exercises that follow.

In 1946 Fred Brazos arrived in Virginia with a strong personality, a good background in electronics, and $300 in cash. He was able to increase this small amount of capital, and five years later he established Brazos Manufacturing,

Inc. In early 1960, at the age of 41, he was president of an organization which in 1959 did over $1.6 million in business.

Brazos Manufacturing, Inc., was a small firm in that part of the rapidly expanding electronics industry that was centered in eastern Virginia. As this industry continued to grow quickly in size, so did the company. In 1956, therefore, the company moved away from eastern Virginia and relocated in the southern part of the state. There the company operated from a new single-story steel and glass plant. Brazos employed about 175 workers, the largest part of whom were women. A significant portion of these employees were also highly skilled.

Brazos' products were known for their precision, and the company had an excellent record for careful, exact work. The tiny machines it produced were so small that highly skilled hands were required to make the precision product needed. Brazos encouraged his employees to be precise and paid them more money when their work was entirely satisfactory.

Adapted from Gayton Germane, 1954

Vocabulary in Context

In the passage above there may be some words that you do not know. The example below shows how you can discover the meaning of a word from its context.

"Precision" is a **noun.** We know this because of the *-ion* ending. In line 14, "precision" follows the verb "known." The products of the Brazos company are "known" for their "precision." The company itself "had an excellent record," or was known, for "careful, exact work." Thus, the company and its products were known for "precision" or "careful, exact work." In line 16, we see that "precision" is used to modify "product." A precision product, therefore, is an exact product. Finally, in line 17, we find an adjective form of the noun "precision," "precise," which also means "exact."

Now do the following exercises.

Exercise 12

In each blank below, write the word from the Reading Exercise passage that has nearly the same meaning as the **boldface** word or phrase in the sentence.

1. The products of the Brazos company were known for their **exactness.**

    ____

2. The electronics industry in eastern Virginia was rapidly **growing in size.**

    ____

3. In 1956, the Brazos company **moved** to the southern part of the state.

   ____

4. A large **part** of Brazos' employees were highly skilled.

   ____

5. By 1951, Fred Brazos had increased his **cash** and established Brazos Manufacturing, Inc.

   ____

6. Brazos' company produced **very small** machines that required highly skilled hands to produce.

   ____

7. Brazos paid his employees more money when they were **exact** in their work.

   ____

Exercise 13

Read the following short passages and select the best answer from the choices given. Circle the letter for the answer you choose.

1. The amount of money required to start a business is increasing every year. The capital needed is also much more in cities than in the country, where costs are very low.

   Capital means

   a. business
   b. money
   c. establish
   d. costs

2. The number of people in the world is expanding very rapidly. As the world population grows in size, cities become larger and more crowded.

   Expand means

   a. number
   b. population
   c. become larger
   d. become more crowded

3. It is becoming more difficult to live by farming, and many farmers are relocating in cities to find new jobs and homes. However, when these farmers become established in their new places, they discover that food and housing cost much more than in the country.

   Relocate means

   a. become difficult
   b. find a new job
   c. discover something new
   d. become established in a new place

4. A large portion of society prefers the traditional values of the culture. Another part, however, desires to change the accepted ways for more modern values. In an ideal society, these two parts are balanced.

Portion means

a. traditional c. value
b. culture d. part

5. Precision of measurement is more difficult in the social sciences than in the physical sciences. For example, we cannot count exactly how much knowledge people have, or measure precisely how happy they are. Since our measurements of qualities such as these do not have exactness, there is always a certain amount of error in them.

   Precision means

   a. exactness c. knowledge
   b. measurement d. error

6. A single person produces a very small percentage of the national product. But even this tiny amount is essential to the economic growth of the entire nation.

   Tiny means

   a. single c. very small
   b. essential d. entire

7. Banks must be very precise in reporting the amounts of money they hold. If customers are not provided with exact figures, they will no longer trust the banks.

   Precise means

   a. amount c. figure
   b. reporting d. exact

Exercise 14

Answer the following questions, based on the Reading Exercise passage.

1. When did Fred Brazos establish Brazos Manufacturing, Inc.?

   ____

2. What was Fred Brazos' position in 1960?

   ____

3. How much business did Brazos Manufacturing, Inc., do in 1959?

   ____

4. What industry was Brazos Manufacturing, Inc., a part of?

   ____

5. Why did Fred Brazos first locate his company in eastern Virginia?

   ____

6. Why did the company leave eastern Virginia?

   ____

7. What two characteristics were shared by most of Brazos' employees?

____

____

8. What did Brazos Manufacturing, Inc., produce?

____

9. How did Fred Brazos encourage his employees to be precise in their work?

____

Lesson 5

How Can Companies Increase Their Capital?

PREREADING ACTIVITIES

A. Discussion Questions

1. If you owned a factory and needed money to buy new equipment, in what ways could you obtain the money?
2. Do you know what a bond is?
3. Can you explain what a stock is?
4. What are the advantages and disadvantages of buying bonds? stocks?

B. Special Vocabulary (Marked "*" in Passage A)

bond	a certificate issued by a company promising to pay back money that has been loaned to it, along with money charged for the money borrowed.
promissory note	a written promise to pay back money owed
interest	moncy charged for borrowing money
principal	the amount of money owed, not including interest
sue	to make a claim against a person or a company in a court of law

stock	a certificate issued by a company assuring ownership in the money and earnings of a company
dividend	a periodic payment of a part of the earnings of a company

C. Guide Questions

As you read Passage A, ask yourself the following questions.

1. What two ways for a company to increase its capital are mentioned in the first paragraph?
2. What other process is discussed in the second paragraph?
3. What process is discussed in the third paragraph?
4. What can a person who buys bonds do if the company does not make payments of interest on time?
5. What does the person who buys stocks receive?
6. Can persons who own stocks help to decide how the company will handle its business?
7. Who takes part in the losses of a company, a person who owns stocks or a person who owns bonds?

NOW READ PASSAGE A. WHEN YOU FINISH READING, ANSWER THE GUIDE QUESTIONS.

READING PASSAGES

How Can Companies Increase Their Capital?

Adapted from Paul A. Samuelson, 1970

Passage A

Companies can increase the **money** with which they run their business in a number of ways. One way is borrowing money, and another way is buying things with the **agreement that payment can be made later.** There are also other processes for **providing money** for use by a company. Two of these processes are described here.

One process the company may use is to issue *bonds. Bonds are a special kind of *promissory note. They are issued in different values, in the **forms of money** used in different countries, such as the pound in England or the mark in Germany. These bonds can easily be **sold again** to other people or to other companies. The company that issues the bonds **promises** to pay a **particular** amount of money as *interest regularly for a certain period of time. This continues until the time when the company has to pay back the *principal of the bond. Payments of principal and interest must be made on time whether the company has been earning money or not. If these payments are not made on time, it means that the company has not **done what it agreed** to do and can be *sued.

Another process companies may use is to issue other forms of promissory notes called *stocks. Bonds and stocks are opposite methods of providing money for a company. The **people who buy stocks** provide money which is **put into and used by** the company. These persons receive a **part** of the **money that is earned** and take part in **deciding** how the company will conduct its business. They must also **take part** in the losses. The people who own stocks receive *dividends only after the company has paid all of its debts to the **people who own bonds.** On the other hand, the persons who own bonds have no right, **according to the law,** to help decide how the company will handle its business, unless it is bankrupt or in danger of becoming so.

NOW GO BACK AND ANSWER THE GUIDE QUESTIONS.

Passage B

Companies can increase their **capital** in a number of ways. Besides borrowing money and buying **on credit,** they can use some other processes of **financing.** Two of these processes are described here.

First, they may issue bonds. Bonds are special kinds of promissory notes which are issued in different values in various **currencies.** They can easily be **resold.** The company issuing the bonds **guarantees** to pay a **specific** amount of money in interest regularly for a certain period of time, until the time when the company has to pay back the principal of the bond. Payments of the principal and interest must be made on time, whether the company has been making earnings or not. If these payments are not made on time, the company has not **fulfilled** its **obligations** and can be sued.

Second, the company may issue stocks. Bonds and stocks are opposite methods of financing. The **stockholders** provide the capital which is **invested** in the business. They have a **share** in the **profits** and in making business **decisions,** but they must also **share** in the losses. The stockholders never receive any dividends until the money owed to the **bondholders** is paid off. On the other hand, unless the company is bankrupt or in danger of becoming so, the bondholders usually have no **legal** control over the decisions of the business.

COMPREHENSION EXERCISES

Exercise 1

Reread Passage B and then answer the questions below.

1. What processes of financing can companies use to increase their capital? Companies can increase their capital by

   a. ______________________ money

   b. ______________________ on credit

   c. ______________________ bonds

   d. ______________________ stocks

2. Which of these processes are described in the passage?

   ____

   ____

3. What sentence in the first paragraph *introduces* these two processes?

   Two______________________ are described ______________________. (l. 3)

This sentence functions as an *introduction* to the topic of the passage.

4. What is the tense of the main verb in this sentence?

   ____

Exercise 2

Answer the following questions, based on Passage B.

1. What process is described in the second paragraph?

   ____

2. What process is described in the third paragraph?

   ____

3. Write the verbs in the blanks below:

   a. Bonds______________________ special kinds of (l. 4)

   b. The company . . .______________________ to pay (l. 6)

   c. Bonds and stocks______________________ opposite methods (ll. 12–13)

d. The stockholders____________________ the capital (l. 13)

e. They____________________ a share in the profits (l.14)

f. The stockholders never____________________ any dividends (ll. 15–16)

g. The bondholders usually____________________ no legal control (l. 18)

These sentences function to express facts and conditions that are *parts* of the process.

4. What is the tense of the main verbs in these sentences?

____

Exercise 3

Reread Passage B and answer the following questions.

1. In line 3, *these processes* refers to ____________________.
2. In line 4, *they* refers to ____________________.
3. In line 5, *they* refers to ____________________.
4. In line 10, *these payments* refers to ____________________.
5. In line 15 *they* refers to ____________________.

In Passage B, the author uses two words to mean nearly the same thing:

6. In line 12, we read "the____________________ may issue stocks."
7. In lines 13–14, we read "invested in the____________________."
8. In this passage "the ____________________" and "the ____________________" have nearly the same meaning: "an organization for conducting business."

Exercise 4

The word *so* often takes the place of another word or phrase.

Example: . . . unless the company is bankrupt or in danger of becoming *so*, ... (l. 17)

In this sentence *so* takes the place of the word *bankrupt.*

In many cases, *so* takes the place of a complete clause.

Example: The newspaper says that it will rain tomorrow, but I don't think *so*.

In this sentence, *so* takes the place of, or replaces, the clause *that it will rain tomorrow*.

Read the sentence below. In the blanks write the word or words that are replaced by *so*.

1. The bottling company hopes to obtain a franchise soon. It will do so when it has the proper equipment.

   ____

2. It is very difficult for some students to understand English grammar. But others do not find it so.

   ____

3. A scatter diagram shows the relationship between two variables. Other kinds of graphs can do so as well.

   ____

4. The article says that China was involved in power politics. However, some historians do not believe so.

   ____

5. If the police trainee is an officer, or is in the process of becoming so, he is given a higher salary.

   ____

VOCABULARY EXERCISES

Exercise 5

Fill in the blanks with words from the list. Each word is used at least once.

capital	financing	obligation
credit	guarantees	profits
currencies	invested	specific
decisions	legal	

Borrowing money and buying on ______________ are ways a company can increase its ______________. Other processes of ______________ a company are the issuing of bonds or stocks. Bonds are special kinds of promissory notes issued in different values in different____________________. A company that sells bonds________________ to pay a________________ amount of money as interest. The company has the________________ to pay the interest and principal on time. Stocks represent the money that a person has________________ in a company. When a company sells stocks, it agrees to give the buyer a share of its________________ and to let that person help make business________________. The bondholder, on the other hand, usually has no________________ right to share in the company's decisions.

Exercise 6

Read each of the definitions below and choose the word from the list that matches the definition. Then write the correct word in the blank.

capital	finance	obligation
credit	guarantee	profit
currency	invest	specific
decision	legal	

1. ________________ the trust or confidence that a company (or a person) will pay its debts
2. ________________ a conclusion or plan of action you reach after you have carefully thought about something
3. ________________ to provide money for use by a company
4. ________________ to place money in order to earn more money
5. ________________ a duty or contract to do something
6. ________________ the money earned by a business or individual after all debts and expenses have been paid
7. ________________ the form of money used by a particular country
8. ________________ of or about the law
9. ________________ to promise to do something
10. ________________ particular or definite
11. ________________ money needed by a company to conduct business

WORD SKILLS

A. The adjective suffixes *-ary* and *-ory*

Example from Passage B: promiss*ory* (l. 4)

The suffixes *-ary* and-*ory* are added to verbs to form adjectives. They mean "relating to" or "connected with."

Examples: *Verb*	*Adjective*
explain	explanatory*
imagine	imaginary*
introduce	introductory*
promise	promissory*

*Note spelling change.

***-ary* and *-ory* are sometimes added to nouns to form nouns.**

Examples: *Noun*	*Noun*
diction	dictionary
honor	honorary

Exercise 7

Fill in each blank below with the *-ary* or *-ory* adjective form for the underlined word.

1. Alicia signed a note that promised that she would pay a certain amount of money.

   Alicia signed a ______________________ note.
2. Professor Aghbar wrote a textbook that introduces the topic of economics.

   Professor Aghbar wrote an ______________________ textbook in economics.
3. It was a report that explained their actions.

   It was an ______________________ report of their actions.
4. Ramon imagined that he earned a profit.

   The profit Ramon earned was ______________________.
5. Prof. Morrison was awarded a degree in honor of his work.

   Prof. Morrison was awarded an ______________________ degree.

B. The noun suffix *-sion*

Example from Passage B: deci*sions* (l. 15)

The suffix *-sion* is added to verbs to form nouns.

Examples: *Verb*	*Noun*
decide	decision*
include	inclusion*
invade	invasion*

*Note spelling change.

Exercise 8

Write the correct verb form of the underlined noun in each of the following sentences.

1. A company must make decisions about what business it will do.

   A company must ______________ what business it will do.
2. The stockholders have permission to help run the business.

   The stockholders are ______________ to help run the business.
3. The company reached the conclusion that it should issue stocks.

   The company ______________ that it should issue stocks.
4. Issuing stocks and bonds are provisions of the company's contract.

   Issuing stocks and bonds are ______________ for in the company's contract.
5. There is an equal division between stockholders and bondholders.

   Stockholders and bondholders are ______________ equally.

DISCOURSE SKILLS

Exercise 9

A *process* is a series of actions or steps that are followed in order to produce a definite result.

Two processes for increasing capital are described in Passage B: (1) issuing bonds and (2) issuing stocks.

1. What is the purpose of issuing bonds and stocks?

   ____
2. Who issues bonds?

   ____

3. Who buys bonds?

____

4. For how long does the company guarantee to pay interest on bonds?

____

5. Until when does the company continue to pay interest?

____

6. Under what conditions can the bondholder sue the company?

____

In the blanks below, number the steps in the process of issuing bonds, in the correct order. Write "1" for the first step.

_______ 7. The company pays interest.

_______ 8. The bondholder buys the bonds.

_______ 9. The company pays back the principal of the bonds.

_______ 10. The company issues the bonds.

Now answer the following questions about the third paragraph.

11. Who issues stock?

____

12. Who provides the capital?

____

13. What is done with the capital?

____

14. When can the stockholder receive dividends?

____

15. What must happen for the bondholders to have legal control of the company?

____

In the blanks below, number the steps or actions in the process of issuing stocks. Write "1" for the first step.

_______ 16. The capital is invested in the business.

_______ 17. The company issues the stock.

_______ 18. The stockholder receives dividends.

_______ 19. The money owed the bondholder is paid off.

_______ 20. The stockholder provides the capital.

Exercise 10

The word *until* introduces the second point in time.

Examples:

Until the end of the nineteenth century, (Second Point in Time)	very few companies issued stocks. (First Point in Time)
Very few companies issued stocks (First Point in Time)	until the end of the nineteenth century. (Second Point in Time)

Read each sentence below. Underline each time expression that indicates the *second* point in time.

1. The company pays interest until the time when it must pay back the principal of the bond.
2. Until the beginning of the new year, the interest rate will stay at 12 percent.
3. A company may issue stocks and bonds until it no longer needs capital.
4. Until last year, the interest rate was quite low.
5. The stockholder must wait until the bondholder is paid off to receive any dividends.
6. The company pays dividends until it is not making earnings.
7. The price of cars will continue to increase until costs can be reduced.

Exercise 11

In the blanks below number the points in time according to the sentences in Exercise 10 above. Write "1" for the first point in time and "2" for the second.

_______ 1. The company pays the interest.

_______ The company must pay back the principal of the bond.

_______ 2. The beginning of the new year.

_______ The interest rate stays at 12 percent.

_______ 3. A company may issue stocks and bonds.

_______ A company no longer needs capital.

_______ 4. Last year.

_______ The interest rate was quite low.

_______ 5. The stockholder must wait to receive any dividends.

_______ The bondholder is paid off.

_______ 6. The company is not making earnings.

_______ The company pays dividends.

_______ 7. Costs are reduced.

_______ The price of cars will continue to rise.

Exercise 12

Answer the following questions, based on Passage B.

1. What phrases in the passage are used to tell the *possible ways* for companies to increase their capital?

   a. Companies _______________ their capital (l. 1)

   b. First, they _______________ bonds (l. 4)

   c. Second, the company _______________ stocks (l. 12)

2. In sentences (a) to (c), circle the modal verbs that indicate *possibility*. Write them below:

   a. _______________

   b. _______________

   c. _______________

These sentences that contain the modals "may" and "can" function to indicate *possibilities* within the process.

Exercise 13

Answer the following questions, based on Passage B.

1. What phrases in the passage are used to indicate a *requirement* in the process?

a. The company ______________________ the principal (l. 8)

b. Payments of . . . interest ______________________ on time (ll. 8–9)

2. In sentences (a) and (b), circle the modal verbs that indicate *requirements*. Write them below:

a. ______________________

b. ______________________

The sentences with a modal of necessity ("must," "have to") function to indicate a *requirement* within a process.

READING EXERCISE

Read the following passage and then do the exercises that follow.

In the stock market a person can be successful and make a fortune one year and another year be financially ruined. Stocks and bonds are bought and sold in the stock and bond markets. Bonds often pay a lower rate of interest than stocks. In addition, bonds mature or become payable much more slowly than do stocks. Even so, bonds offer greater safety for the buyer. This is because companies must guarantee to pay bondholders a fixed rate of interest whether they make a profit or not. Bonds are, therefore, generally considered a form of long-term security. This means that they are a safe investment over a long period of time. However, they may not be redeemable right away. In other words, owners of bonds may have to wait a long time before they can exchange their bonds for money.

The interest paid by stocks rises and falls with the economy. During times when the cost of living is rapidly becoming greater, stocks are usually a better investment than bonds. This is because they pay a much higher interest rate than do bonds under these conditions. When economic conditions are not good, however, bonds are generally a better investment. This is because the interest paid by bonds is fixed at a certain rate when they are issued and does not change. Because of the relationship between the economy and the performance of stocks and bonds, when people are not sure about economic conditions, they may hesitate before buying anything. They prefer to wait and see what happens to the prices and rates of interest of stocks and bonds before investing their money.

Adapted from Paul A. Samuelson, 1970

Vocabulary in Context

The example below shows you how you can discover the meaning of a word from its context.

"Redeemable" is an **adjective.** We know this because of the *-able* ending.

Also, "redeemable" comes after a form of the verb "be," and words following this verb are often adjectives. In Lesson 3 we learned that the suffix *-able* is added to verbs. We can see that the base of "redeemable" is the verb "redeem." From this, we know that "redeemable" means "able to be redeemed." The word modified by "redeemable" is "they," and since this refers to "bonds," we know that bonds may not be able to be redeemed. Next, we try to find a word or phrase that means the same as the verb "redeem." In lines 9 and 10 we find the phrase "in other words," which tells us that what follows means nearly the same as the sentence with "redeemable." In this sentence, we are told that owners of bonds may have to wait a long time before they can exchange their bonds for money. That is, owners of bonds may not be able to exchange their bonds for money right away. From this, we can see that "redeem" means "exchange for money."

NOW DO THE FOLLOWING EXERCISES.

Exercise 14

In each blank below, write the word from the Reading Exercise passage that has nearly the same meaning as the **boldface** word or phrase in the sentence.

1. He was not a very clever businessman and he lost all his money. **In terms of his finances,** he was ruined.

   ____

2. Bonds **become payable** much more slowly than do stocks.

   ____

3. Even though bonds often pay a lower **percent of** interest, they offer greater safety for the buyer.

   ____

4. Bonds are a good investment **over a long period of time.**

   ____

5. People who are worried about the **safety** of their investment usually buy bonds.

   ____

6. One is not **able to exchange** bonds **for money** right away.

   ____

7. When economic conditions are uncertain, some people **are slow to decide** before buying or selling stocks or bonds.

   ____

8. Bonds **usually** pay a lower rate of interest than stocks. However, in **most cases** bonds are a more secure investment.

    ____

Exercise 15

Read the following short passages and select the best answer from the choices given. Circle the letter for the answer you choose.

1. Bonds are generally a safer investment than stocks. This is because companies must guarantee payments of interest to bondholders, whether they make a profit or not. In most cases, however, bonds mature more slowly and are less redeemable than stocks.
    Generally means
    a. safer
    b. less redeemable
    c. more slowly
    d. in most cases
2. Bonds often pay a lower interest rate than do stocks. Even though bonds pay a lower percent of interest, they offer greater safety for the buyer.
    Rate means
    a. percent
    b. lower
    c. greater safety
    d. interest
3. Over a long period of time, bonds are a safe investment. They also give good long-term financial returns.
    Long-term means
    a. bonds
    b. safe investment
    c. long period of time
    d. financial returns
4. Bonds mature more slowly than stocks. They become payable only after a long period of time.
    Mature in this passage means
    a. become payable
    b. become ruined
    c. become slower
    d. long period
5. He hesitated before buying a new car. He imagined that if he waited a few days the price would come down.
    Hesitate means
    a. buy
    b. wait
    c. price
    d. think
6. The check was not redeemable right away. She had to wait for the bank to accept the check before she was able to cash it.
    Redeemable means
    a. able to be cashed
    b. right away
    c. able to check
    d. wait

7. The company lost all of its money in the stock market. It was financially ruined.

   Financially means

   a. ruined
   b. lost
   c. in terms of money
   d. in terms of the stock market

8. Bonds offer the buyer more security than stocks. With bonds the buyer knows there is safety in the long-term investment.

   Security means

   a. buyer
   b. long-term
   c. stocks
   d. safety

Exercise 16

Answer the following questions, based on the Reading Exercise passage.

1. When are stocks usually a better investment than bonds?

   ____

2. Where are stocks and bonds bought and sold?

   ____

3. Which generally pay a higher rate of interest, stocks or bonds?

   ____

4. Is the interest rate on stocks fixed?

   ____

5. What is one reason people hesitate before buying stocks or bonds?

   ____

Lesson 6

Recent Economic Growth

PREREADING ACTIVITIES

A. Discussion Questions

1. How much better is our life now than that of people who lived 200 years ago?
2. Describe some changes that have taken place in the past 200 years that have improved the way people live.
3. What has made these changes possible?
4. Will it be possible to continue to improve the way we live in the next 200 years? Why or why not?

B. Special Vocabulary (Marked "*" in Passage A)

agriculture	the science or practice of raising plants or animals useful to civilization; farming
revolution	the overthrow of a government; causing a change in government or in the form of government

C. Guide Questions
As you read Passage A, ask yourself the following questions.

1. Which paragraph introduces the topic of the passage?
2. Which paragraph provides some historical background?

3. Which paragraph describes recent developments?
4. Which paragraph discusses future possibilities?
5. In the last 200 years, what changes have occurred?
6. What have these changes caused?
7. What do some people think will happen to the earth's energy and material?
8. Does the author agree with these people?
9. According to the author, why should we not be afraid?

NOW READ PASSAGE A. WHEN YOU FINISH READING, ANSWER THE GUIDE QUESTIONS.

READING PASSAGES

Recent Economic Growth

Adapted from Carl H. Madden, 1976

Passage A

The industrial societies have **produced a large amount** of **material** during the past two centuries. The economic **progress** has been **worthy of notice.** During this period of time, which is short **in relation to** other periods, greater changes in people's living conditions have **happened** than in the thousands of years which **went before.**

From about 8000 B.C., when the **period** of *agriculture began, to 1776 A.D., which was the beginning of the American *Revolution, people **became** hardly any richer at all. The Americans of 1776 got energy from the same **places** as Romans of 1 A.D.[1] Both could travel about the same short distance in a day. Both **earned** the same **amount of money every year** and **lived** the same **number of years.**

During the last two centuries the **number of people** in the world has **become** 6 times **larger,** the **amount** of material **produced** in the world **during a year** has become 80 times larger, and the distance a person can travel has gone up 1,000 times. There has also been much recent progress in art, culture, learning, and science. Such changes have **caused** an increase in **speed** in the **making of materials** and have caused the economy **to grow.**

People who study economics are afraid that within the next 100 to 150 years the earth's **energy and material** will become very **difficult to find.**

[1]People who lived in the ancient city of Rome, which was the capital of the Roman Empire (27 B.C.–395 A.D.)

Their fears are **based** partly **on good reasons,** but we should not be afraid. Industrial civilization **changes** to make use of new knowledge. By advancing knowledge, we not only create new **types** of energy and material, but we also find ways to **use** them **less.** Advanced modern knowledge can provide food for the hungry people of the world and improve **how well they live.**

Passage B

The industrial societies have been **extremely productive** during the last two centuries. The economic **advance** has been **remarkable.** During this **relatively** short period of time, greater changes in people's living conditions have **occurred** than in the thousands of years which **preceded.**

From about 8000 B.C., when the agricultural **era** of the human race began, to 1776 A.D., the beginning of the American Revolution, people **grew** hardly any richer at all. The Americans of 1776 used the same energy **sources** as the Romans of 1 A.D. Both the ancient Romans and the Americans of 200 years ago could travel about the same short distance in a day. Both had about the same **annual income** and the same **life span.**

During the past 200 years the world **population** has **increased** 6 times, the **annual** world **output** has increased 80 times, and the distance a person can travel has gone up 1,000 times. There has also been much recent progress in art, culture, learning, and science. Such changes have **led to** a high **rate** of **production** and **growth** of the economy.

Economists fear that within the next 100 to 150 years, the earth's **resources** will become very **scarce.** Their fears are partly **justified,** but we should not be afraid. Industrial civilization **adapts to** new knowledge. By advancing knowledge, we not only create new **forms** of resources, but we also find ways to **economize** their use. Advanced modern knowledge can feed the hungry people of the world and improve their **standard of living.**

COMPREHENSION EXERCISES

Exercise 1

Reread Passage B and then answer the following questions.

1. What is the first, or earliest point in time mentioned in the passage?

   about ____________________ B.C.

2. What happened at this time?

   ____

3. What is the second point in time in the passage?

   ____________________ A.D.

4. What people lived at this time?

____

5. What is the third point in time in the passage?

______________ A.D.

6. What event happened at this time?

____

7. During the time period between the first and third points in time, what was the general condition of people?

____

8. What phrase refers to this period, which began in

______________ and ended in ______________?

____

9. What conditions were the same during the *second* and *third* points in time?

The Americans of 1776 and the ancient Romans of 1 A.D. both

a. ______________________________

b. ______________________________

c. ______________________________

d. ______________________________

10. How many years after the American Revolution was this passage written?

____

11. What time expression tells you this?

____

Exercise 2

Reread Passage B and then answer the following questions.

1. In lines 2 to 3 *this relatively short time period* refers to

____

2. In the last sentence of the first paragraph, some information has been left out, or omitted. What did "the thousands of years" precede?

____

3. In the last two sentences of the second paragraph, some information has also been omitted. The word *both* in lines 8 and 9 refers to

____

4. In line 14 *such changes* refers to
   a. ____________________
   b. ____________________
   c. ____________________
   d. ____________________
5. What three different phrases does the author use to refer to the same period of time?
   a. during ____________________
   b. During ____________________
   c. During ____________________
6. In line 17, *their* refers to ____________________.
7. In line 20, *their* refers to ____________________.
8. In line 21, *their* refers to ____________________.

VOCABULARY EXERCISES

Exercise 3

Fill in the blanks with the words from the list. Each word is used at least once.

adapt	output	remarkable
annual	population	resources
income	rate	sources
occurred	relatively	

Since 1776, the industrial societies have become more and more productive. The advance in the way wealth is used is ____________________.

Greater changes have ____________________ in people's living conditions in the last two centuries than in the thousands of years preceding.

The ancient Romans and the Americans of 1776 used the same energy ____________________. Both had the same ____________________ ____________________ and the same life span. In the ____________________ short period of time since 1776, the ____________________ world ____________________ has increased 80 times and the world ____________ has increased 6 times. Such changes have led to a high ____________ of production and use of the world's ____________.

Economists tell us that within the next 100 to 150 years, the earth's ____________ may become very scarce. But industrial civilization is able to ____________ to new knowledge. Advanced knowledge can feed the hungry people of the world and improve the quality of their life.

Exercise 4

Choose the word from the list that has nearly the same meaning as a phrase in parentheses and write that word in the blank.

adapt	output	remarkable
annual	population	resources
income	rate	source
occur	relative	

1. (energy and material that can be used when needed) ____________
2. (every year) ____________
3. (the amount made or produced) ____________
4. (the number of people or living things in an area) ____________
5. (how fast something happens) ____________
6. (worthy of notice) ____________
7. (a place or origin) ____________
8. (the money someone earns) ____________
9. (to take place; to happen) ____________
10. (to change to suit a specific situation or use) ____________
11. (in relation to or compared with) ____________

WORD SKILLS

A. The verb suffix *-ize*

Example from Passage B: econom*ize* (l. 20)

The suffix *-ize* is added to nouns and adjectives to form verbs. The suffix *-ize* usually means "to make" or "to become."

Examples: *Noun*	*Verb*
economy	economize*
industrial	industrialize
public	publicize
special	specialize
summary	summarize*

*Note spelling change.

Exercise 5

Write the correct form of the *-ize* verb for the underlined words in each sentence below.

1. Please make a summary of this report for our meeting.

   Please ______________________ this report for our meeting.
2. You should make the arrangements formal as soon as possible.

   You should ______________________ the arrangements as soon as possible.
3. You should make the company's policies more public.

   You should ______________________ the company's policies.
4. We didn't think Mr. Harris could make his plans real, because he wasn't very economical with his money.

   We didn't think Mr. Harris could ______________________ his plans, because he wasn't very economical with his money.
5. The theories of J. M. Keynes have done much to make the study of economics popular.

   The theories of J. M. Keynes have done much to ______________________ the study of economics.

B. The agent noun suffix *-ist*

Example from Passage B: econom*ists* (l. 16)

The suffix *-ist* is added to nouns and adjectives to form agent nouns.

Examples: *Noun*	*Agent Noun*
drama	dramatist*
economy	economist*
industrial	industrialist
special	specialist

*Note spelling change.

Exercise 6

Fill in the blanks with the correct agent noun ending in *-ist.*

1. Prof. Samuels studied economics at Harvard University and is now a leading ______________________.
2. The humor of Will Rogers was greatly appreciated by the people of the United States. He was one of the great ______________________ of his time.
3. When Vladimir Horowitz plays the piano, the music lovers of the world listen. He is a truly great ______________________.
4. Many of the developing countries of the world are beginning to become industrial. There are not many ______________________ in these countries now, but they are increasing in number.
5. Dr. Maynard has a special interest in Chinese history. She is one of the most famous ______________________ in her field.

Many agent nouns ending in *-ist* have corresponding *-ize* verbs.

Examples:

Noun	*Verb*
capitalist	capitalize
nationalist	nationalize
specialist	specialize

C. The adjective suffix *-ive*

Example from Passage B: product*ive* (l. 1)

The suffix *-ive* is usually added to verbs to form adjectives.

Examples:

Verb	*Adjective*
create	creative*
decide	decisive*
include	inclusive*

Some words ending in *-ive* can be either nouns or adjectives.

Examples:

Verb	*Noun or Adjective*
correct	corrective
operate	operative*
relate	relative*

*Note spelling change.

Exercise 7

Fill in the blanks with the *-ive* form of the underlined word in each sentence below.

1. The vote of women may decide the next election.

   The vote of women may be ______________ in the next election.
2. The prime minister's speech impressed many people.

   The prime minister's speech was very ______________.
3. The president is elected to office.

   The office of president is ______________.
4. Current economic developments indicate that prices will continue to increase.

   Current economic developments are ______________ of a continued increase in prices.
5. The scientist collected data that allowed her to describe the process of economic growth.

   The scientist collected ______________ data about the process of economic growth.

DISCOURSE SKILLS

Exercise 8

Reread Passage B and then answer the following questions.

1. From the beginning of the American Revolution until the present, what changes have occurred?

   a. ______________

   b. ______________

   c. ______________

   d. ______________

   e. ______________

   f. ______________

   g. ______________
2. Did these changes occur only in the past?

   ____

3. During what other time might changes such as these also occur?

____

Changes that happen during one time period and continue into another time period are called *trends*.

4. What *past trends* continue into the present?
   a. industrial societies continue to be ______________________________
   ____
   b. the economic advance continues to be ______________________________
   ____
   c. ____
   d. ____
   e. ____
   f. ____
   g. ____
5. To what present conditions have these changes led?
   a. a high rate of ____________________
   b. growth of ____________________
6. What other changes are happening at the present time?
   a. industrial civilization ______________________________
   ____
   b. knowledge ______________________________
   ____
   c. we create ______________________________
   ____
   d. we ______________________________
   ____
7. Are these changes occurring only in the present?

   ____
8. During what other time period might these changes happen?

   ____

9. Does the author think these changes will continue into the future?

____

10. What *present trends* will continue into the future?

    a. industrial civilization will ________________

    ____

    b. knowledge will ________________

    ____

    c. we will ________________

    ____

    d. we will ________________

    ____

11. Economists fear that ________________
12. When do they think this will happen? ________________
13. Does the author think this will happen? ________________
14. What *present trends* will keep this from happening?

    a. industrial civilization will ________________

    ____

    b. ________________

    c. ________________

    d. ________________

15. If the economists are correct, what can happen *in the future?*

    ____

16. If the author is correct, what can happen *in the future?*
    Advanced modern knowledge can

    a. feed ________________

    b. improve ________________

Exercise 9

In Passage B, the author indicates a point in time and also shows that a period of time begins at that point.

Example: *From* about 8000 B.C. . . . to 1776 . . . (ll. 5–6)

Words such as *after, afterward, from,* and *since* are frequently used to show a point in time at which a time period begins.

In each sentence below, underline the words that show the point at which a time period begins. Write the point in time in the blank.

1. ______________ Since about 1800, life expectancy has more than doubled in many countries of the world.
2. ______________ From about 1870, birth rates began to decrease in most Western countries.
3. ______________ After the 1930s, the drop in birth rates increased.
4. ______________ The birth rate increased rapidly after World War II.
5. ______________ America has experienced a steady fall in the birth rate since about 1957.
6. ______________ After 1960, birth rates in Western European countries fell sharply.
7. ______________ The birth rate decreased during World War II but increased rapidly afterward.
8. ______________ From the year 1 A.D. to 1776, the life expectancy was about the same.

Exercise 10

Read each sentence below and indicate whether it describes a *point* in time or a time *period.* Write either "point" or "period" in each blank.

1. ______________ Within the past 200 years, the world population has increased six times.
2. ______________ The agricultural era of the human race began about 8000 B.C.
3. ______________ People grew hardly any richer in the thousands of years before 1776.
4. ______________ Since about 1776, the distance a person can travel has gone up a thousand times.
5. ______________ Between 1 A.D. and 1776 the sources of energy people used did not change very much.
6. ______________ The American Revolution began in 1776.
7. ______________ The industrial societies have been extremely productive in the last two centuries.
8. ______________ The Americans of 1776 had about the same income as the Romans of 1 A.D.

9. ______________________ Within the next 100 to 150 years natural resources might become very scarce.

10. ______________________ Science will develop new forms of resources between now and the twenty-first century.

Exercise 11

Time Periods and Conditions

A *time period* begins and ends with a *point in time*. Words such as *during, within, between,* and *since* are used with time expressions to indicate time periods.

The economic *conditions* described in Passage B take place during time periods. Conditions can occur in the past, the present, and the future. Conditions can also continue from one time period into another.

A. Conditions in the past

A condition that began *and ended* in the past is indicated by the use of the *past tense*.

Example: From about 8000 B.C. . . . to 1776 . . . people *grew* . . .

- From about 8000 B.C. — Beginning of Time Period
- to 1776 — End of Time Period
- people *grew* — Condition

B. Conditions in the past and the present

A condition that began in the past and *continues* into the present is indicated by the use of the *present perfect tense*.

Example:
societies *have been* extremely productive during the last two centuries

- societies *have been* extremely productive — Condition
- during the last two centuries — Time Period

C. Conditions in the present

Conditions that are true at present are indicated by the use of the *present tense*.

Example: Industrial civilization *adapts* . . .

D. Conditions in the future

Conditions that will begin in the future are indicated by the use of the verbs *will, shall, can, may,* and *might*.

Example:

within the next 100 to 150 years — Beginning of Time Period

the earth's resources *will* become . . . — Condition

Read the sentences below and underline each time expression and each verb. Then indicate when the conditions in the sentence occur, using the symbols below. Write the correct symbol in the blank before each sentence.

PAST = occurring in the past *only*
PA-PRES = beginning in the past and continuing into the present
PRES = occurring in the present
FUT = occurring in the future *only*

________ 1. For many years, economists have been interested in trends in population growth.

________ 2. Supply and demand created patterns of agricultural activities in the past.

________ 3. Since 1929 most nations have developed plans for economic growth.

________ 4. Modern science may reduce the death rate faster than it can increase the food supply.

________ 5. Many countries use employment and development plans to increase economic growth.

________ 6. Within a few years many natural resources will be replaced by cheaper manufactured materials.

________ 7. Land reform has helped economic development in some countries in the past few centuries.

________ 8. Before World War II, economic development resulted mainly from foreign investments.

________ 9. In the modern world, a system of taxes is often used to achieve greater equality of wealth.

_____________ 10. In general, wages and income have risen greatly since about 1880.

READING EXERCISE

Read the following passage and then do the exercises that follow.

There is much discussion today about whether economic growth is desirable. At an earlier period, our desire for material wealth may have been justified. Now, however, this desire for more than we need is causing serious problems. Even though we have good intentions, we may be producing too much, too fast.

Those who criticize economic growth argue that we must slow down. They believe that society is approaching certain limits on growth. These include the fixed supply of natural resources, the possible negative effects of industry on the natural environment, and the continuing increase in the world's population. As society reaches these limits, economic growth can no longer continue, and the quality of life will decrease.

People who want more economic growth, on the other hand, argue that even at the present growth rate there are still many poor people in the world. These proponents of economic growth believe that only more growth can create the capital needed to improve the quality of life in the world. Furthermore, they argue that only continued growth can provide the financial resources required to protect our natural surroundings from industrialization.

This debate over the desirability of continued economic growth is of vital importance to business and industry. If those who argue against economic growth are correct, the problems they mention cannot be ignored. To find a solution, economists and the business community must pay attention to these problems and continue discussing them with one another.

Adapted from Carl H. Madden, 1976

Vocabulary in Context

The example below shows you how to discover the meaning of a word from its context.

"Limit" is a **noun.** We know this because the plural form, "limits," follows the word "these" in line 10. "Limits" is the object of the verb "is approaching" in line 7, and in line 10 it is the object of the verb "reach." So a limit is something that can be approached and reached. But what happens when a limit is reached? According to this passage, once certain limits are reached, "economic growth can no longer continue." These limits, therefore, mark a point when economic growth ends. From this we can see that a "limit" is a "point beyond which something cannot continue."

NOW DO THE FOLLOWING EXERCISES.

Exercise 12

In each blank below, write the word from the Reading Exercise passage that has nearly the same meaning as the **boldface** word or phrase in the sentence.

1. Those who **argue against** economic growth are sometimes not liked by the business community.

   ____

2. More capital is **needed** for the new equipment than the company can provide.

   ____

3. Some economists believe that continued economic growth is **essential** to the well-being of society.

   ____

4. The leaders of the business community agreed to continue their **discussion** of the advantages and disadvantages of economic growth.

   ____

5. It is impossible to **refuse to pay attention to** the problems of economic growth.

   ____

6. The **people who want** more economic growth believe that such growth can provide the solution to many of today's problems.

   ____

7. The fixed supply of natural resources marks **a point beyond which** economic growth **cannot continue.**

   ____

8. Our natural **surroundings** are in danger of being destroyed by industry.

   ____

Exercise 13

Read the following short passages and select the best answer from the choices given. Circle the letter for the answer you choose.

1. People often ignore new ideas. If they don't understand these new ideas, they refuse to give any attention to them.
   Ignore means to
   a. understand
   b. not understand
   c. refuse to give attention to
   d. believe
2. Oil is of vital importance to the world. It is used both at home and in industry. It is a necessary part of everyone's life.
   Vital means
   a. oil and industry
   b. a part of life
   c. useful
   d. necessary
3. Several famous economists will debate the topic of economic growth today. These experts regularly argue and consider the problem in order to find a solution.
   Debate means to
   a. continue
   b. find
   c. argue and consider
   d. grow
4. Anyone who intends to criticize the economic growth of industry must be well informed. Arguing against current industrial practices must be based on well-established facts.
   Criticize means to
   a. grow economically
   b. argue against
   c. establish facts
   d. be well informed
5. A large amount of capital will be required to finance plans to protect our natural surroundings from the effects of industrialization. These financial resources will be needed to pay for costly equipment and processes.
   Required means
   a. surrounded
   b. protected
   c. needed
   d. paid
6. Proponents of economic growth argue that there are no limits to how fast the economy can grow. People who argue for an economic slowdown, however, believe that the rate of economic is growth is limited by the supply of natural resources, possible negative effects on the environment, and an increasing population.
   Proponents means
   a. limits to growth
   b. natural resources
   c. negative effects
   d. people who argue for something
7. There is a limit on the number of ways in which a company can increase its capital. However, there is no end to the amount of time a company can use in raising money.
   Limit means
   a. end
   b. number of ways
   c. amount of time
   d. money

8. The world of international business is a very difficult environment to adapt to. It often takes several years for one to become used to the procedures and surroundings in different countries.

   Environment means

   a. international
   b. surroundings
   c. business
   d. countries

Exercise 14

Answer the following questions, based on the Reading Exercise passage.

1. What three limits on economic growth are mentioned in the passage?

   ____

   ____

   ____

2. What may happen as these limits are reached?

   ____

3. How might more economic growth be able to protect the environment?

   ____

4. Why is the debate about economic growth vital to business and industry?

   ____

5. How might a solution be found?

   ____

   ____

Lesson 7

The Quality of Labor

PREREADING ACTIVITIES

A. Discussion Questions

1. What skills are required for the job that you hope to obtain?
2. How much and what kind of training is required for that job?
3. Have you ever had a job that required no training?
4. How might you classify jobs according to the skills and training they require?
5. Give some examples of these different kinds of jobs.

B. Special Vocabulary (Marked "*" in Passage A)

weld	to join two pieces of metal by heating them
canal	a waterway made by people, generally used for shipping or travel
entrepreneur	a person who organizes and controls a business enterprise

C. Guide Questions
As you read Passage A, ask yourself the following questions.

1. How do economists define *labor*?
2. What three groups of laborers are mentioned?

3. What qualities show differences among these groups?
4. What kind of worker is someone who makes tools?
5. Which of the three kinds of work is the most specific?

NOW READ PASSAGE A. WHEN YOU FINISH READING, ANSWER THE GUIDE QUESTIONS.

READING PASSAGES

The Quality of Labor

Adapted from Geoffrey Whitehead, 1982

Passage A

To an economist, labor is the supply of human resources which can be used in the production of goods and services. Both labor and laborers can be classified into three **groups:** skilled, **partly skilled,** and unskilled. There are certain **qualities** which **are particular to** each group and which **show the differences** between it and the other two groups. These qualities are the degree of skill and training needed for the job and **how specific** a task the worker performs.

Skilled labor is of two kinds. The first kind has **expert knowledge** in a particular area, like **making tools** or printing. The second kind has received **advanced** education **and special** training. Doctors, teachers, and lawyers are examples of this kind of skilled labor.

A partly skilled worker is a person who has gained a very large amount of skill over a very limited **number** of activities. Such workers can be trained very quickly. Someone who *welds in a plant where **automobiles** are **put together** is an example. **In the same way,** one **person who makes** business machines believes that a person can be **completely** trained to operate one of these machines in two days.

Unskilled workers, or workers who are not skilled, as their name **suggests,** need **hardly any** specialized training. Skills can be **obtained** on the job itself, and as the workers **become** used to the work, they become more **productive.** For example, when the *canals were built in Britain, and later when the **railroads** were laid, the *entrepreneurs who built them found that it took a full year for strong healthy farm boys to become diggers. These young men had to use their energy economically so that they could work long hours without tiring. **A lot** of special training was not **needed,** but the strong body and character that the job required was not produced in a single day.

In classifying labor, it is also important to know how specific the task is. **In general,** it **is usually true** that skilled workers' tasks are more specific than are those of partly skilled or unskilled workers. Skilled workers usually do only the work for which they have special skill or training. **For example,** a dentist must be employed in dentistry in order to use his or her special skills. For a dentist to work in the fields planting corn would be a waste of these skills. Of course, it might **help** the dentist **a great deal** to find out about the life of a farmer, but this experience cannot **take the place** of the productive use of the dentist's services in taking care of people's teeth. A welder in an automobile factory is an example of a less specific kind of worker. This worker might be **just as** useful repairing cars or welding the steel framework of a new building.

NOW GO BACK AND ANSWER THE GUIDE QUESTIONS

Passage B

To an economist, labor is the supply of human resources which can be used in the production of goods and services. Labor can be classified into three **types:** skilled, **semiskilled,** and unskilled. Each of these types has certain **characteristics** which **distinguish** it from the other two. These distinguishing characteristics are the degree of skill and training required of the worker and the **specificity** of the task performed.

Skilled labor is labor which either has **expertise** in a particular skill, like **toolmaking** or printing, or which has received **professional** training, such as doctors, teachers, and lawyers.

A semiskilled laborer is a person who has reached a very high degree of skill over a very limited **range** of activities. Such labor can be trained very quickly. A welder in a **motor vehicle assembly** plant is an example. **Similarly,** one **manufacturer** of business machines believes that an operator can be **fully** trained in two days.

Unskilled labor, as its name **implies,** requires **little** specialized training. Skills can be **acquired** on the job itself, and as the laborers **grow** used to the work, they become more **efficient.** For example, when the canals were built in Britain, and later when the **railways** were laid, the entrepreneurs who built them found that it took a full year for strong healthy farm boys to become diggers. These young men had to learn to use their energy economically so that they could work long hours without tiring. Although **a great deal** of specialized training was not **necessary,** the strong body and character that the job required were not produced in a single day.

The idea of specificity is also important in classifying labor. **Generally speaking,** skilled labor **tends** to be more specific than semiskilled or unskilled labor; skilled laborers usually perform only those tasks for which they have special skill or training. **For instance,** a dentist must be employed in dentistry in order to use his or her special skills. For a dentist to work in the fields planting corn would be a waste of these skills. Of course, it may **do** the dentist **a world of good** to find out about the life of a farmer, but this would not **substitute** for the efficient use of the dentist's services in caring for people's teeth. A welder in an automobile factory is a less specific type of labor. This laborer might be **equally** useful repairing cars or welding the steel framework of a new building.

COMPREHENSION EXERCISES

Exercise 1

Reread Passage B and then answer the questions below.

Paragraph 1

1. What three types of labor are mentioned?

   ____

   ____

   ____

2. What are the distinguishing characteristics of these three types of labor?

   ____

   ____

Paragraph 2

3. What characteristic distinguishes skilled labor?

   either ____________________________________

   or ______________________________________

4. What are two examples of labor that has expertise in a particular skill?

   ____

   ____

5. What are three examples of labor that has professional training?

   ____

   ____

   ____

Paragraph 3

6. What are the distinguishing characteristics of semiskilled labor?

   ____

   ____

7. What are two examples of semiskilled labor?

____

____

Paragraph 4

8. What are the distinguishing characteristics of unskilled labor?

____

____

9. What is an example of unskilled labor?

____

Paragraph 5

10. What is another important characteristic for classifying labor?

____

11. What is the most specific type of labor?

____

12. What characteristic permits skilled laborers to perform their specific tasks?

____

13. What example is given to show the degree of specificity of the task of a skilled laborer?

____

14. What example is given to show the degree of specificity of the task of a semiskilled laborer?

____

Exercise 2

Answer the following questions, referring back to Passage B.

1. In line 3, *these types* refer to types of _______________.
2. In line 11, *such labor* refers to _______________ labor.
3. In line 13, *similarly* introduces another example of

_______________.

An author frequently repeats a word throughout a passage in order to help connect the different parts of the passage.

Example: The word *labor* is used in every paragraph and helps to provide a connection among the different paragraphs in the passage.

4. What other words are repeated in the same or similar forms in the passage?

    ____

    ____

Sometimes an author uses synonyms to show connections among the different parts of a passage.

5. What synonyms for the word *task* (l. 6) are used in the passage?

    ______________________ (l. 16)

    ______________________ (l. 17)

6. What synonym for the word *worker* (l. 5) is used in the passage?

    ______________________ (l. 10)

VOCABULARY EXERCISES

Exercise 3

Read each definition below and choose the word from the list that best matches each definition. Then write that word in the blank.

acquire	efficient	range
assembly	imply	substitute
characteristic	manufacturer	tend
distinguish	professional	

1. ______________________ to obtain by one's own efforts or behavior
2. ______________________ to make noticeable or different
3. ______________________ amount of variation; extent
4. ______________________ to be likely; usual
5. ______________________ related to a job requiring advanced education and special training
6. ______________________ the putting together of parts; a gathering together of people

7. ____________________ a person or firm that produces things on a large scale
8. ____________________ to suggest
9. ____________________ producing effectively with little waste in time, effort, or money
10. ____________________ typical outward appearance; quality or behavior typical of a group, class, or individual
11. ____________________ to put or use in place of another

Exercise 4

Fill in each blank with a word from the list. Each word is used only once.

acquired	efficient	range
assembly	implies	substitute
characteristics	manufacturer	tend
distinguish	professional	

One ____________________ of airplanes has opened up a new ____________________ plant in California. This new plant employs ____________________ people such as engineers who design the airplanes and semiskilled workers who perform a wide ____________________ of activities. Some of the employees have just graduated from technical schools, but most employees have been ____________________ from the company's large plant in Georgia, which closed three months ago because of labor problems. The workers ____________________ to like this new plant because it is clean and ____________________ and the company pays the workers excellent salaries. There is a very low rate of absence in this new plant. Even if someone is absent, it is not a serious problem because one worker can usually ____________________ for another. The efficiency expert at the plant feels that a low absentee rate ____________________ good working conditions for the workers.

The company's profits have been quite good so far this year. The company believes that this is due not only to the quality of its product, but also to the ____________________ of its employees, which are their willingness to work overtime, their efficiency, and their pride in their work. These qualities ____________________ these employees from other airplane assembly plant workers, who usually have high absentee rates and little pride in their work.

WORD SKILLS

A. The prefix *semi-*

Example from Passage B: *semi*skilled (l. 3)

Semi- **is a prefix meaning "partly," "not fully," or "half."** ***Semi-*** **can also mean "twice in a specified period of time."**

Examples:

Word	*Meaning*
semiannual	twice a year
semiautomatic	partly automatic
semipublic	not completely open to the public
semiweekly	twice a week

Exercise 5

Fill in the blanks below with a word beginning with *semi-*. Be sure to use the correct part of speech.

1. Although Ramon doesn't play tennis professionally, he's quite good and does win some money from it.

   I'd say Ramon is a ______________________ tennis player.
2. Gelatin is neither completely solid nor completely liquid; it's a

   ______________________.
3. Their new car isn't fully automatic; it's ______________________.
4. You can't say she's completely literate because she can't write her own language.

   Since she can read a little, we could say she's ______________________.
5. Although the public cannot play golf at this club without being a member, anyone can eat at the club's dining room.

   This club is ______________________.

B. The adjective suffix *-y*

Example from Passage B: health*y* (l. 19)

The suffix ***y-*** **is usually added to nouns to form adjectives. It can mean "full of," "characterized by," or "having."**

Examples:

Noun	*Adjective*	*Meaning*
dirt	dirty	full of dirt
luck	lucky	having luck

Exercise 6

Change the underlined words to adjectives ending in *-y*.

1. The area was characterized by rocks, hills, and dust.

   The area was ____________, ____________, and ____________.

2. When they were young their family had wealth, but now their only income is the dividends from a few stocks.

   When they were young their family was ____________, but now their only income is the dividends from a few stocks.

3. We couldn't eat the bread we bought because it had mold on it.

   We couldn't eat the bread we bought because it was ____________.

4. I saw the great length of the book and decided not to read it.

   The book was very ____________, so I decided not to read it.

5. The robber's feelings of guilt caused him to tell about the crime.

   Because the robber felt ____________, he told about the crime.

The suffix *-y* is sometimes added to nouns or verbs to form nouns. The suffix *-y* can mean "quality or condition," "act of doing something," or "a collective body."

Examples:	*Verb*	*Noun*	*Meaning*
	assemble	assembly*	the act of assembling
	recover	recovery	the act of recovering
	unite	unity*	the condition of being united

*Note spelling change.

Exercise 7

Write the noun formed with *-y* from the underlined word in each sentence below.

1. A police officer delivered the stolen car to the owner.

   The ____________ of the stolen car was made by a police officer.

2. They discovered the new element at the university.

   Thc ____________ of the new element was made at the university.

3. If nations unite against war, the world will be a better place.

   If there is ______________________ among nations against war, the world will be a better place.

4. I think it will be difficult to recover the money.

   I think the ______________________ of the money will be difficult.

5. David injured himself in an automobile accident.

   David received an ______________________ in an automobile accident.

DISCOURSE SKILLS

Exercise 8

In Passage B, certain words and phrases are used to signal or indicate which things are being given as examples. Fill in the blanks below with the word or phrases that signal examples.

1. ______________________ toolmaking or printing (l. 8)
2. ______________________ doctors, teachers, and lawyers (l. 9)
3. A welder . . . ______________________ (l. 12)
4. ______________________, when the canals were built (ll. 17–18)
5. ______________________, a dentist must be employed (ll. 27–28)

Some of the words and phrases used to signal examples are *for example, for instance, like,* and *such as.* Examples can also be signaled by phrases like *type of* and *kind of.*

Exercise 9

In Passage B several general statements, or *generalizations,* are made. Some of these generalizations are followed by specific examples. The examples *exemplify,* or illustrate, and make clearer the meaning of the generalization.

1. A generalization given in paragraph 1 is that the distinguishing characteristics of three types of labor are

   ____

   ____

In paragraphs 2 and 3 several examples are given of the *first* of these two characteristics. Complete the chart below, filling in the blanks with the correct distinguishing characteristics, signals, and examples.

Type	Distinguishing Characteristics	Signal	Specific Examples
Skilled labor	________	________	________
	________		________
	________		
	or		
	________	________	________
	________		________
	________		________
	________	________	________
Semiskilled labor	________		
	________		
	________		________
	________		
	________		________

In paragraphs 2 and 3, examples are given in a list.

***Listing* is the simplest form of exemplification.**

Exercise 10

In paragraph 4, a situation is described as an example of the generalization given earlier in the passage.

***Describing a situation* is another form of exemplification.**

Fill in the blanks below, based on paragraph 4.

1. Type of labor described: ________
2. Example of labor: ________
3. Signal of example: ________

Situational Example:

4. canals ________
5. railways ________

Distinguishing Characteristics of Type of Labor	Characteristics of Situation
6. requires ______ ______	a. ______ ______ was not necessary.
7. training can be ______ ______	b. it took ______ ______ ______
	c. the strong body and . . . required ______ ______
8. as the laborers ______ ______	d. these young men ______ ______ ______ ______
9. they become ______	

Exercise 11

In paragraph 1, a generalization is made about the distinguishing characteristics of labor. The first distinguishing characteristic of labor is the degree of skill and training required of the worker. The *second* distinguishing characteristic of labor is

1. ______

This generalization is repeated in paragraph 5:

2. ______ is also important in classifying labor.

How does the idea of specificity apply to skilled labor?

3. ______
4. ______

In paragraph 5, two situations are described as examples of the specificity of labor. These situations are of two kinds:

Actual situation:	A situation that is true or that actually happens.

Hypothetical situation: A situation that is possible or that might happen but has not actually happened yet.

Hypothetical situations are often signaled by words like *if, probably,* and *possibly* or with modals like *would, could, may,* and *might.*

Fill in the blanks below. In the first column write "A" if it is an actual situation; if it is a hypothetical situation, write "H."

Type of Situation	Situation	Type of Labor Exemplified
5. ______	a ______________ must be employed in ______________ in order to use his special skills	a. ______________
6. ______	For a ______________ to work in the fields planting corn ______________ a waste of these skills. it ______________ the ______________ a world of good . . . but this ______________ not substitute for the use of his services	
7. ______	A ______________ in an automobile factory ______________ a less ______________ type of labor.	b. ______________
8. ______	This laborer ______________ be equally ______________ cars or ______________ the steel . . .	

Exercise 12

Each of the sentences below contains a generalization, or a general class, and one or more examples of that generalization or general type. In each of the sentences below, do the following:

a. Underline the phrase that is a generalization or a general type.
b. Underline *twice* the word or words that are examples.
c. Circle the word or words that signal(s) the example.

1. Doctors, teachers, and lawyers are examples of skilled labor.
2. Several kinds of financing, such as stocks and bonds, are available to companies.
3. The manufacture of transistors is one example of standardization in production.
4. Prices generally rise as demand increases, such as has happened with the price of real estate in the past few years.
5. There is always a small part of the population that is unable to work, such as very young children or sick persons.
6. Some types of labor, such as the control and management of a business, are highly specialized.
7. First-year students study such subjects as mathematics, chemistry, and English.
8. Kitimat, in British Columbia, is an excellent example of the location of an industry near a source of power.
9. Industries are usually located near places that provide easy transportation. For instance, the whole port area of Rotterdam, Holland, is covered with a complex of industrial projects.
10. Neurologists, pediatricians, and oculists illustrate the high degree of specialization in the medical profession.

READING EXERCISE

Read the following passage and then do the exercises that follow.

Specialization of tasks permits each person to use to the best advantage any particular skills or resources he or she may have. Even in a primitive economy, people learn that, rather than having everyone do everything in an average way, it is better to start a division of labor. For instance, it is better for fat people to do the fishing, thin people to do the hunting, and smart people to make the medicine—each trading his or her goods for the goods he or she needs. Specialization also increases productivity. An example of this is pin making. One individual could at best make a few dozen imperfect pins per day. But when a small group of people is divided according to their different skills, each person can perform the same simple operation repeatedly and the group can make thousands of perfect pins each day. Specialization also prevents the wasteful production of extra tools that would be necessary if each person had to perform many different tasks. Finally, specialization also saves time lost going from one job to another.

Adapted from Geoffrey Whitehead, 1982

Exercise 13

In each blank below, write the word from the Reading Exercise passage that has nearly the same meaning as the **boldface** word or phrase in the sentence.

1. This tribe of people is **at a very early stage of social development** and has no modern tools or clothing.

   ____

2. This factory produces 10,000 cars **each** month.

   ____

3. The tools made by these machines are all of the same **high quality**, and **have no faults.**

   ____

4. The employees were given jobs **in a way that suited** their training and experience.

   ____

5. The company hired an efficiency expert to help increase **the amount of work produced** by the workers.

   ____

6. Physical strength is **a characteristic that will help a person succeed** as a coal miner.

   ____

7. Skilled laborers are able to perform very detailed **procedures**.

   ____

8. People whose work is of **poor quality** and **full of mistakes** will not be able to keep their jobs.

   ____

Exercise 14

Answer the following questions, based on the Reading Exercise passage.

1. What three examples are given to exemplify the specialization of labor in a primitive society?

   ____

   ____

   ____

2. What advantage of specialization is exemplified by pin making?

   ____

3. Are more or less tools required with the specialization of labor?

   ____

4. Why is this so?

   ____

   ____

5. Why does specialization save time?

   ____

   ____

Lesson 8

Exchanging Surpluses through the Money System

PREREADING ACTIVITIES

A. Discussion Questions

1. What goods produced in other countries do you regularly use?
2. Choose one product that is produced in another country as an example, and try to describe how it gets from the producer to you.
3. What do you think the producer receives in exchange for the goods?
4. Why doesn't the producer keep the goods for his or her own use?
5. What do you give in exchange for the product?
6. What people are involved in getting the goods from the producer to you?

B. Special Vocabulary (Marked "*" in Passage A)

ore	rock or earth from which metal can be obtained
smelt	to separate metal from ore by melting
sailor	someone who works on a ship
auction	to sell goods at a public sale to the person who offers the highest price
wholesaler	a person who sells goods in large quantities to merchants or retailers

pulp	soft, moist, shapeless material, especially that obtained from trees and used in the manufacture of paper
retailer	a person who sells goods individually or in small quantities directly to people who use the goods

C. Guide Questions

As you read Passage A, ask yourself the following questions.

1. What does every productive member of society do?
2. What must be done with the extra goods or services that are produced?
3. What process is described in this passage?
4. What example of this process is given?
5. What part does money have in this process?
6. What is the most important part of the process?

NOW READ PASSAGE A. WHEN YOU FINISH READING, ANSWER THE GUIDE QUESTIONS.

READING PASSAGES

Exchanging Surpluses through the Money System

Adapted from Geoffrey Whitehead, 1982

Passage A

In general, every productive member of society specializes in some kind of employment. Each person produces more things or provides **more** services **than are needed** for his or her own use. These **extras** have to be **traded** so that everyone can satisfy his or her needs. Money is a part of the process which **helps** this trade **happen.**

A simple **example** of this process is the **buying** of a **box** of tea by a lawyer who has been performing her useful services for, let us say, ABC Company. For these services she receives an average salary. She uses some of this salary to buy a box of tea. The tea was grown in Sri Lanka on a **farm** financed by British and Sri Lankan capital. The tea was then **sent** to the United States in boxes. The **inside** of these boxes was **covered** with aluminum paper. The aluminum paper was produced in Canada from *ore *smelted in Kitimat, in British Columbia. The **method** used **to carry** the tea was a British ship whose *sailors were Indian. The tea was *auctioned in New York and bought by a *wholesaler. **After some time** the wholesaler packed it in paper **containers.**

These containers were made from *pulp produced in Labrador. Next, the wholesaler sold the tea to a *retailer. The retailer then sold it to the lawyer.

When the lawyer bought the tea, her only thought was, "Do I have enough money to buy the tea?" But money was not the most important **part of the process.** Money actually **hid** what was really happening. All over the world a **large number** of people in **many** specialized **jobs** were **taking care of** the lawyer's needs. They did this in **return** for her services.

NOW GO BACK AND ANSWER THE GUIDE QUESTIONS.

Passage B

In general, every productive member of society specializes in some kind of employment. The **surpluses** produced by this specialization have to be **exchanged** if everyone is to satisfy his or her needs. Money plays a part in **promoting** these exchanges of surpluses.

A simple **illustration** of this process is the **purchase** of a **package** of tea by a lawyer who has been performing her useful services for, let us say, ABC Company. For these services she receives an average salary. She uses some of this salary to purchase a package of tea. The tea was grown in Sri Lanka on a **plantation** financed by British and Sri Lankan capital. The tea was **shipped** to the United States in boxes **lined** with aluminum paper produced in Canada from ore smelted in Kitimat, in British Columbia. The **transportation** used was a British ship whose sailors were Indian. The tea was auctioned in New York and purchased by a wholesaler who **eventually** packed it in **cartons** made from pulp produced in Labrador. The wholesaler then sold the tea to a retailer, who sold it to the lawyer.

At the time of the purchase, the lawyer's only thought was whether she had enough money for the tea. Money, however, was not the most important **factor.** Money actually **obscured** what was really happening. All over the world an **army** of people in **a hundred** specialized **occupations** were **attending** to the lawyer's needs in **exchange** for her services.

COMPREHENSION EXERCISES

Exercise 1

Reread Passage B and then answer the questions below.

1. What is the first generalization made in the passage?

____

____

2. What is the second generalization made in the passage?

____

____

3. What process is the passage mainly about?

____

____

4. What example of this process is given in the passage?

____

____

5. What phrase signals this example?

____

6. Is this example an actual or a hypothetical situation?

____

7. Does the lawyer actually work for ABC Company?

____

8. What phrase tells you this?

____

9. This example also illustrates a third generalization made in the first paragraph. What is this generalization?

____

____

Exercise 2

Answer the following questions by referring to Passage B.

1. In line 2, *this specialization* refers to specialization in ________________.
2. In line 4, *these exchanges* refers to exchanges of ________________.
3. In line 5, *this process* refers to ________________________.
4. In line 6 we see the phrase "*a* lawyer" and in line 15 the phrase "*the* lawyer." Why is the definite article "the" used in the second phrase?

   ____

5. To whom does the phrase "the wholesaler" in line 14 refer?

   ____

The definite article *the* is used with common nouns when they have been mentioned earlier in a passage.

6. In line 19 we see the word "army." Does the author really mean an actual army in this sentence?

   ____

7. What does the author mean by the word "army" in this passage?

   ____

Authors do not always use words with their actual, or *literal,* meanings. Sometimes they use words or phrases *figuratively*. A word or phrase that is used figuratively has a quality that the author wants to emphasize.

Example: "an *army* of people . . . " (l. 19)

Here the author does not *literally* mean an army, but wants to emphasize the meaning "a large group."

8. What does the author mean by the phrase "a hundred" in line 19?

   ____

VOCABULARY EXERCISES

Exercise 3

Read each of the definitions below and choose the word from the list that matches the definition. Then write that word in the blank.

eventually	factor	occupation	purchase
exchange	obscure	promote	surplus

1. ______________________ a person's trade, profession, or job
2. ______________________ to give something in return for something else
3. ______________________ to help organize and begin
4. ______________________ to hide; to make unclear
5. ______________________ an amount more than what is needed or used
6. ______________________ to buy

7. ______________________ a part of a process or condition

8. ______________________ in the end; at some future time

Exercise 4

Fill in each blank below with the correct word from the list. Each word is used only once.

eventually	factor	occupations	purchase
exchanged	obscures	promote	surplus

A long time ago people simply ______________________ their own goods or services for other goods or services. As contact between different parts of the world became easier, trading involved many different people and many exchanges. ______________________ money was used to ______________________ the exchange of ______________________ goods and services.

Although money is a ______________________ in promoting exchanges, it actually ______________________ what is really happening. The goods or services we ______________________ come to us as a result of many individuals working in many different specialized ______________________.

WORD SKILLS

In Lesson 1, you learned about the noun suffix *-ation*. Go back and review Word Skills Section A, on page 26. In this lesson, you will learn about two more forms that the suffix *-ation* can take.

A. The noun suffix *-ation* with verbs ending in *-ize* and *-ify*

Example from Passage B: specializ*ation* (l. 2)

The suffix *-ation* can be added to verbs ending in *-ize*. The e at the end of the verb is omitted.

Examples:

Verb	*Noun*
civilize	civilization
organize	organization
realize	realization

When the suffix *-ation* is added to verbs ending in *-ify*, it takes the form *-cation*. The *y* at the end of the verb is changed to *i*.

Examples: *Verb*	*Noun*
certify	certification
classify	classification
exemplify	exemplification

Exercise 5

Complete each sentence below, using the correct noun form of the underlined verb.

1. "Is that country completely <u>industrialized</u>?"

   "No, but ________________ is moving very quickly."
2. If you <u>qualify</u>, you will be accepted for the job.

   If you have the proper ________________, you will be accepted for the job.
3. The countries were <u>classified</u> according to their economic resources.

   The ________________ was made according to the economic resources of the countries.
4. "What is causing this country to <u>urbanize</u>?" "There is no simple answer,

   since ________________ depends upon many factors."
5. All the newspapers have been <u>notified</u> of the election.

   ________________ of the election has been given to all the newspapers.

B. The adjective suffix *-ful*

Example from Passage B: use*ful* (l. 6)

The suffix *-ful* is added to nouns to form adjectives. It usually means "full of," "characterized by," or "having."

Examples: *Noun*	*Adjective*	*Meaning*
beauty	beautiful*	full of beauty
pain	painful	having pain; causing pain
use	useful	having use

*Note spelling change.

The suffix *-ful* is sometimes added to verbs to form adjectives.

Examples: *Verb*	*Adjective*	*Meaning*
forget	forgetful	having poor memory
help	helpful	giving help; having the ability to help

Exercise 6

Write the adjective formed with *-ful* from the underlined word in each sentence below.

1. The Adams Company didn't have any success in exporting its goods to other countries.
   The Adams Company wasn't ______________ in exporting its goods to other countries.
2. They hope that they will do better next year.
   They are ______________ that they will do better next year.
3. You always seem to forget something important.
   You are very ______________ of important things.

C. The noun suffix *-age*

Example from Passage B: pack*age* (l. 5)

The suffix *-age* is often added to verbs to form nouns. It can mean "act," "condition," "amount," "number," or "cost of."

Examples:	*Verb*	*Noun*	*Meaning*
	pass	passage	the act of passing from one place to another; the place through which one passes
	stop	stoppage*	the act of stopping something
	waste	wastage*	the act of wasting; material that is wasted

*Note the spelling change.

The suffix *-age* is sometimes added to nouns.

Examples:	*Noun*	*Noun*	*Meaning*
	mile	mileage	the number of miles traveled
	post	postage	the cost of sending something by mail (post)

Exercise 7

Fill in each blank with the correct word from the list below.

package	marriage
stoppage	mileage
wastage	postage

1. "Where did they get married?"

   "The ________________________ took place at St. Paul's church."
2. "How long do they plan to stop working?"

   "The work ________________________ is expected to last for two months."
3. "Do you think energy is being wasted by the public?"

   "Yes, I think there is a great deal of energy ________________________ by the public."
4. "How much will it be to post this letter to Australia?"

   "The ________________________ will be 85 cents."
5. "How many miles has this car traveled?"

   "The ________________________ is 19,000 miles."
6. "Did you pack those papers yet?"

   "Yes, and I took the ________________________ to the airport."

DISCOURSE SKILLS

Exercise 8

The situational example in Passage B is a *specific process* described in time order. This process consists of several *primary steps.* These steps are *primary,* or the most important, to the process because they directly involve the handling of the tea.

1. Below is a list of these *primary* steps. Number them in their order of occurrence, beginning with "1" for the first step. Number simultaneous steps with the same number.

   _______ a. The package of tea was purchased by the lawyer.

   _______ b. The tea was grown in Sri Lanka.

   _______ c. The tea was purchased by the wholesaler.

   _______ d. The wholesaler sold the tea to the retailer.

   _______ e. The tea was shipped to the United States.

   _______ f. The retailer sold the tea to the lawyer.

   _______ g. The tea was auctioned in New York.

   _______ h. The wholesaler packed the tea in cartons.

Several of the primary steps in the process depend on or are related to *secondary steps,* which do not directly involve the handling of tea.

Example:	*Primary Step*	*Secondary Step*
	The tea was grown in Sri Lanka.	(The plantation) was financed.

2. In the left-hand column below, several primary steps are listed, and in the right-hand column, several secondary steps. Find the primary step that is related to each secondary step. Then write the letter for the primary step in the blank in front of the secondary step.

Primary Steps

a. The tea was grown in Sri Lanka.
b. The tea was shipped to the United States.
c. The tea was shipped in boxes lined with aluminum paper.
d. The wholesaler packed the tea in cartons.
e. The lawyer uses some of her salary to purchase a package of tea.

Secondary Steps

_______ The aluminum paper was produced in Canada.
_______ The pulp was produced in Labrador.
_______ The plantation was financed by British and Sri Lankan capital.
_______ The transportation used was a British ship.
_______ The lawyer performs her services.

_______ The cartons were made from pulp.
_______ The lawyer receives her salary.
_______ The ship's sailors were from India.
_______ The ore was smelted in Kitimat.

3. Below is a list of the primary and secondary steps in the process. Within each group, number the steps in the order of their occurrence.

_______ a. The lawyer receives an average salary.

_______ The lawyer performs her useful services.

_______ The lawyer uses some of her salary to purchase a package of tea.

_______ b. The tea was grown on a plantation in Sri Lanka.

_______ The plantation was financed by British and Sri Lankan capital.

_______ c. The aluminum paper was produced in Canada.

_______ The tea was shipped in boxes lined with aluminum paper.

_______ The ore was smelted in Kitimat.

_______ d. The wholesaler packed the tea in cartons.

_______ The pulp was produced in Labrador.

Exercise 9

Reread Passage B and then answer the questions below.

1. What takes place in *each step* in the process described in the situational example?

   ____

2. What promotes this?

   ____

3. What does the lawyer receive in exchange for her services?

   ____

4. What does the lawyer give the retailer in exchange for the package of tea?

   ____

These exchanges are mentioned specifically. They are stated *explicitly*, or clearly. However, information about some of the exchanges, and the part played by money in them is not mentioned. Information about these exchanges is only implied, or *implicit*. Below is a list of exchanges that occur in the situational example. Some are explicitly stated; others are implicit. In the blank before each exchange, write "EXP" if it is explicitly stated and "IMP" if it is implicit.

_______ 5. The Indian sailors receive salaries for their work on the ship.

_______ 6. The retailer pays the wholesaler money for the tea.

_______ 7. The wholesaler exchanges money for the cartons.

_______ 8. The lawyer receives a salary in exchange for her services.

_______ 9. The plantation receives capital from British and Sri Lankan financiers.

_______ 10. The wholesaler pays money for the tea.

_______ 11. The ship owner receives a fee for shipping the tea.

_______ 12. The lawyer pays the retailer for the tea.

_______ 13. The producer of aluminum paper receives money for the aluminum paper.

Exercise 10

In Passage B the author states that "an army of people in a hundred specialized occupations" were involved in the example. Some of these occupations are stated explicitly, while others are implicit. Below is a list of occupations that are either explicit or implicit in the example. In each blank below, write "EXP" if the occupation is explicitly stated and "IMP" if it is implicit.

_______ 1. plantation owner

_______ 2. Indian sailor

_______ 3. British and Sri Lankan financiers

_______ 4. Sri Lankan farmer

_______ 5. smelter of aluminum ore

_______ 6. tea auctioneer

_______ 7. wholesaler

_______ 8. producer of aluminum paper

_______ 9. lawyer

_______ 10. retailer

11. List some other occupations that you think are implicit in the example.

____

____

Exercise 11

Read the following passage and then do the exercise that follows.

To an economist, production is the creation of either goods or services. Three main types of production can be distinguished: primary, secondary, and tertiary. Primary production is the production of goods made available by nature. Trees are a natural resource; a wood cutter, or lumberjack, and a sawmill worker are examples of occupations that are classified as primary production.

Secondary production is the production of goods which are made from the natural products of primary production. A builder, for example, uses the wood cut by the lumberjack and sawed by the sawmill worker to make buildings. The occupation of builder, therefore, is classified as secondary production.

Tertiary production is the production of services. These services are of two types: personal and commercial. Personal services satisfy people's needs by giving personal attention such as that provided by doctors, police officers, teachers, and entertainers. Commercial services, on the other hand, are not directly personal but form part of an organization. Examples of such services are bankers, transport drivers, and wholesalers.

Based on the definitions in the passage, fill in the chart below with examples of occupations which are classified as primary, secondary, or tertiary production. Include the occupations listed as well as others you may know of. You may have to use your dictionary to look up some of the occupations.

Occupations

coal miner	retailer	decorator
farmer	psychologist	wholesaler
exporter	transport driver	tailor
detective	sawmill operator	stockbroker
carpenter	engineer	potter
teacher	police officer	oil driller

Types of Production

THE PRODUCTION OF GOODS		*THE PRODUCTION OF SERVICES*	
		Tertiary Production	
Primary Production	*Secondary Production*	*Commercial Services*	*Personal Services*
lumberjack	builder	banker	doctor

READING EXERCISE

Read the following passage and then do the exercises that follow.

Until the exchange of goods or services in a society becomes too complex, simple trade can usually be carried on by barter. This is the direct exchange of goods or services for other goods or services, and it may present quite serious problems for the people trading.

The first problem is that each person must want what the other person has. Suppose that Mr. Jones has cows and Mr. Smith has wheat and that Mr. Jones wants some of Mr. Smith's wheat. If Mr. Smith does not want a cow, barter may not be possible. He could, of course, give Mr. Jones some wheat and wait until Mr. Jones has something that he wants.

Even when each person wants what the other has, they may not be able to agree on a fair exchange. Is a cow worth one sack of wheat or ten? A great deal of time can be wasted trying to equate the values of the goods. The second problem, then, is the difficulty of deciding equal values of the goods to be traded.

The third problem is that large items may be indivisible. Let's say that Mr. Jones' cow is worth two sacks of wheat. What is one sack of wheat worth? If Mr. Jones only wants one sack of wheat, he may need to persuade Mr. Smith to carry over part of the transaction until later, unless he is prepared to divide his cow in half.

Because of these problems, the barter system is no longer used in societies which have developed specialized methods of production. The large number of exchanges necessitated by specialization, as well as their complexity, make a money system of trade essential.

Adapted from Geoffrey Whitehead, 1982

Exercise 12

In each blank below, write the word from the Reading Exercise passage that has nearly the same meaning as the **boldface** word or phrase in the sentence.

1. Specialized occupations **make** a large number of exchanges **necessary.**

    ____

2. Large items cannot be traded directly for goods of lesser value, since such items **cannot be divided.**

    ____

3. In many cases, it is not possible to **make** the value of one item **equal to** the value of another.

    ____

4. An individual can sometimes **directly exchange** his or her services for goods produced by someone else.

    ____

5. A money system of trade greatly facilitates the **act of conducting** business.

    ____

6. **By talking** with the workers, Ms. Hamilton was able to **make** them do their best in completing the project.

    ____

7. When occupations are highly specialized, the production of goods can be **made up of many different and interrelated parts.**

    ____

Exercise 13

Answer the following questions, based on the Reading Exercise passage.

1. What three problems with the barter system are discussed in the passage?

    ____

    ____

    ____

2. What example is given for the problem of equating values of the items to be bartered?

    ____

3. Which two problems might be solved by carrying over part of the transaction until later?

    ____

    ____

4. Where is the barter system no longer used?

    ____

5. Why is this so?

    ____

    ____

6. What system has replaced barter?

    ____

Lesson 9

Japan's Control of Relations with Multinational Companies

PREREADING ACTIVITIES

A. Discussion Questions

1. What companies can you think of that conduct business and have bases of operation in many different countries?
2. What kind of agreements for conducting business do you think such companies have with various individual countries?
3. In what areas do such companies conduct business? (agriculture? electronics?)
4. Are there any areas where individual countries might want to limit the business conducted by such companies? Why these areas?

B. Special Vocabulary (Marked "*" in Passage A)

multinational	conducting business and having bases of operation in many different countries

C. Guide Questions
As you read Passage A, ask yourself the following questions.

1. What are two legal methods for countries to obtain specialized knowledge?

2. Among what group does Japan hold a high position?
3. What industries does Japan try to keep foreign companies from entering?
4. Do many other countries have conditions similar to those in Japan?
5. Why may Japan find its present method of operation less effective than in the past?

NOW READ PASSAGE A. WHEN YOU FINISH READING, ANSWER THE GUIDE QUESTIONS.

READING PASSAGES

Japan's Control of Relations with Multinational Companies

Adapted from Raymond Vernon, 1971

Passage A

For many countries, there are two legal **methods** for obtaining **the specialized knowledge of how to apply science to industry:** to permit *multinational companies to conduct business **inside the country** and to use agreements for obtaining **legal permission** for local companies to act as representatives of multinational companies. Japan **holds** a high **position** among nations that have **tried hard** to keep companies **owned by foreigners** out of industries which are connected with national defense and is **often mentioned** as an **example** showing that a policy **such as this** is **practical.** In this **instance,** multinational ownership of companies operating in Japan is not important for the efficient **exchange** of information about how to apply science to business and industry. The use of agreements for obtaining legal permission is just as efficient.

For more than 100 years, Japan has **regularly** spent **a great deal** of money and a **large amount** of human resources to obtain the knowledge of how to apply science to industry. Japan's ability to **arrange business agreements** for such information has been **made stronger** by the fact that most of the information Japan wanted was not very secret. Japan's position has also been **made stronger** by the fact that the market **inside** Japan was large. By offering multinational companies **a way to reach** this market, Japan could encourage them to grant permissions to Japanese-owned companies to sell their products. **In addition,** Japan's **labor force** was **able to read and write,** and it **worked carefully and regularly,** so it was **able** to **put to use** the information it acquired. Finally, multinational companies based in America and Europe, who were **possible** grantors of permissions, thought that Japanese companies might take a large share of the world market if they were not **controlled** by agreements requiring legal permissions.

Japan may be the **only** country where all the conditions of this **kind** occur together. For this reason, the example of Japan may not actually **show** that agreements for legal permissions are just as efficient as multinational ownership. In fact, Japan may be finding that this method of operation is less effective than in the past. This is because her needs for specialized knowledge from outside Japan now include information which belongs to only a few companies and which is more **secret. In addition,** Japan's need to sell her goods and services to other countries is becoming more important than the need to control the market inside Japan. In the past Japan had the power to arrange business contracts with foreign companies because of her ability to control their **contact with** markets inside Japan. Now, however, this power is becoming weaker because of Japan's need to sell her goods and services to other countries.

NOW GO BACK AND ANSWER THE GUIDE QUESTIONS.

Passage B

For many countries there are two legal **means** for obtaining **technology:** to permit multinational companies to conduct business **within their borders** and the use of **licensing** agreements. Japan **ranks** high among the nations that have **gone to some lengths** to keep **foreign-owned** companies out of industries connected with national defense, and the **case** of Japan is **commonly cited** for the idea that **such** a policy is **feasible.** In this **case,** multinational ownership is not important for the efficient **transfer** of technological information between nations; the use of licensing agreements is just as efficient.

For over a hundred years Japan has **consistently** spent **large sums** of money and **considerable** human resources in an effort to obtain technology. Her ability to **negotiate** has been **strengthened** by the fact that most of the technology she wanted was not very secret. Japan's position has also been **strengthened** by the fact that her **internal** market was large, so that **access** to this market could be offered to multinational companies as an incentive for them to grant licenses. **Besides,** Japan's **work force** was **literate** and **disciplined,** so it was **capable** of **applying** the information it acquired. Finally, American and European companies, who were **potential** licensers, felt that the Japanese companies might take a large share of the world market if they were not **limited** by licensing agreements.

Conditions of this **sort,** coming together in one nation, may well be **unique,** and the case of Japan may therefore not actually **demonstrate** that licensing is just as efficient as multinational ownership for the transfer of technology. In fact, Japan may be finding this method of operation less effective than in the past, as her needs for outside technology now require information which belongs to only a few companies and is more **closely held. Fur-**

thermore, her need to use the markets of other countries is beginning to weaken the negotiating power she once had because of her control of **access** to her internal market.

COMPREHENSION EXERCISES

Exercise 1

Reread Passage B and then answer the questions below.

1. What two methods for the transfer of technological information are mentioned in the first paragraph?

 ____

 ____

2. What is Japan cited as an example of?

 ____

 ____

3. What is the main generalization of the first paragraph?

 ____

4. What generalization is made in the first sentence of the third paragraph?

 ____

 ____

5. Does this generalization agree with the generalization made in the first paragraph?

 ____

Exercise 2

Answer the following questions by referring to Passage B.

1. In line 2, *their* refers to ______________________________.
2. In line 6, *such a policy* refers to ______________________________

 ______________________________.
3. In line 16, *them* refers to ______________________________.
4. In line 19, *they* refers to ______________________________.
5. In line 21, *conditions of this sort* refers to ______________________________

 ______________________________.

6. In line 24, *this method of operation* refers to ______________________________

____.

In lines 8–9, we read that "the use of licensing agreements is just as efficient." This means that licensing agreements are just as efficient as *some other method* for *doing something*. The author does not need to state this explicitly, because this information has already been mentioned in the passage.

7. What other method is as efficient as the use of licensing agreements?

____

8. What are these methods efficient for doing?

____

VOCABULARY EXERCISES

Exercise 3

Read each of the definitions below and choose the word from the list that matches the definition. Then write that word in the blank.

access	disciplined	negotiate
capable	feasible	potential
cite	internal	technology
considerable	license	unique
demonstrate	means	

1. ______________________ possible, but not yet true or in existence
2. ______________________ inside; within
3. ______________________ quite large in amount or degree
4. ______________________ specialized knowledge about the application of science to industry
5. ______________________ written statement giving legal permission
6. ______________________ trained and acting according to specific rules or procedures
7. ______________________ the only one of its kind
8. ______________________ to discuss in order to reach an agreement

9. ____________________ the right to enter or use; a way of approaching something
10. ____________________ able to be done; practical
11. ____________________ to prove clearly by showing evidence
12. ____________________ to mention or refer to as an authority or example
13. ____________________ competent; having ability
14. ____________________ method or way of doing something

Exercise 4

Fill in each blank below with the correct word from the list. Each word is used only once.

access	disciplined	negotiate
capable	feasible	potential
cited	internal	technology
considerable	licensing	unique
demonstrate	means	

Japan is often ____________________ as an example that a policy of trying to keep foreign-owned companies out of industries connected with national defense is ____________________. In Japan's case, the use of ____________________ agreements is an effective ____________________ for the transfer of information.

For many years Japan has spent ____________________ money and resources to obtain ____________________. Japan's power to ____________________ has been strengthened because most of the information she wanted was not secret. Also, Japan's ____________________ market was large, so that ____________________ to it could be used as an effective bargaining point. Because Japan's work force was literate and ____________________, it was ____________________ of applying the information it acquired. Finally, American and European companies, who were ____________________ licensers, felt that Japanese companies needed to be limited by licensing agreements.

For all of these conditions to exist in one nation may be ________________________, and the case of Japan may not actually ________________________ that licensing is just as effective as multinational ownership for the transfer of technology.

WORD SKILLS

A. The prefix *trans-*

Example from Passage B: *trans*fer (l. 7)

The prefix *trans-* is added to bases to mean "across," "from one place to another," "beyond," or "above." It is usually added to adjectives or verbs.

Examples:	*Base*	*Word*	*Meaning*
	act	transact	to do or conduct
	ship	transship	moving from one ship to another

Exercise 5

For each sentence below, choose the word from the list that has the same meaning as the underlined word or phrase. Then write that word in the blank.

transatlantic	transmit
transform	transplant
translate	transport

1. The first person to fly an airplane alone across the Atlantic Ocean was Charles Lindbergh.

   The first person to make a ________________________ plane flight alone was Charles Lindbergh.
2. To change electrical energy from one form into another requires a special device.

   A special device is required to ________________________ electrical energy.
3. When the company moves its offices to Venezuela, it will move its equipment and documents by truck and by ship.

   When the company moves its offices to Venezuela, it will ________________________ its equipment and documents by truck and by ship.

4. Professor Hooshmand plans to change the language of the book from English to Farsi.

   Professor Hooshmand plans to ______________________ the book from English into Farsi.
5. With modern technology it is possible to send information quickly from one place to another by telephone or radio.

   With modern technology it is possible to ______________________ information quickly by telephone or radio.
6. In the spring, Mr. Gray will move some of his rose plants from one part of his garden to another.

   In the spring, Mr. Gray will ______________________ his roses to another part of his garden.

B. The noun suffix *-logy*

Example from Passage B: techno*logy* (l. 1)

The noun suffix *-logy* is added to bases to mean "the science," "theory or study of," or "the body of knowledge about" something.

Examples: *Word*	*Meaning*
biology	the study of living things
geology	the study of the earth

Exercise 6

Combine each of the bases below with the suffix *-logy* and then use these words to fill in the blanks.

Base	Meaning
anthropo-	human
ideo-	idea
meteor(o)-	weather; climate
method(o)-	procedure for doing something
psycho-	of the mind; mental

Word	Meaning
1. ______________________	the study of mental processes
2. ______________________	the study of the development of human culture

3. ______________________ the study of the earth's weather
4. ______________________ a group of ideas that characterizes a person or group
5. ______________________ a group of procedures that characterizes a particular method

C. The prefix *multi-*

Example from Passage B: *multi*national (l. 2)

The prefix *multi-* means "many" or "more than one." It is added to nouns and adjectives.

Examples: *Base*	*Word*	*Meaning*
purpose	multipurpose	having more than one purpose
source	multisource	having more than one source

Exercise 7

Fill in each blank with the word from the list that has the same meaning as the underlined word or phrase,

multicolored multiracial multiuse
multiform multistage

1. The United Nations represents people from many races.

   The United Nations is a ______________________ organization.
2. Some economic processes happen in many stages.

   Some economic processes are ______________________.
3. The flags of most countries have many colors.

   The flags of most countries are ______________________.
4. Plastic is a substance that can be made into many forms.

   Plastic is a ______________________ substance.
5. Petroleum is a source of products that have many uses.

   Petroleum is a ______________________ resource.

D. The verb suffix *-en*

Examples from Passage B: strength*en*ed (l. 12)
weak*en* (l. 28)

The suffix *-en* is added to adjectives and nouns to form verbs. Verbs ending in *-en* usually mean to "make," "cause," "be," or "have the quality of" the base form.

Examples:	*Base*	*Verb*	*Meaning*
	dark	darken	to make or become dark
	length	lengthen	to make or become long
	weak	weaken	to make or become weak

Exercise 8

Complete each sentence below with the correct *-en* verb form of the underlined words.

1. The economy has <u>become weak</u> in the last six months.

   The economy has ________________________ in the last six months.
2. His skin has <u>become dark</u> because he spent many days in the sun.

   His skin has ________________________ because he spent many days in the sun.
3. The company had to <u>increase the length</u> of its working time because it was falling behind in production.

   The company had to ________________________ its working time because it was falling behind in production.
4. This street should be <u>made wider</u> because there have been so many accidents here.

   This street should be ________________________ because there have been so many accidents here.
5. Expectations for a successful solution to the problem <u>became high</u> when a meeting between the two prime ministers was arranged.

   Expectations for a successful solution to the problem

   ________________________ when a meeting between the two prime ministers was arranged.
6. Dr. Malcolm asked her secretary to <u>make the letter shorter</u>.

   Dr. Malcolm asked her secretary to ________________________ the letter.

DISCOURSE SKILLS

Exercise 9

Reread Passage B and then answer the following questions.

1. What generalization introduces the topic of the passage?

   ____

   ____

2. Of what idea is Japan cited as an example?

____

____

3. What generalization is given in the last sentence of paragraph 1?

____

____

Paragraph 2 gives statements as examples that support the generalization made in the last sentence of paragraph 1.

4. What statements in paragraph 2 support this generalization?

a. ____

b. ____

c. ____

d. ____

e. ____

Paragraph 3 presents a *countergeneralization* or a generalization that is the opposite of the generalization made at the end of paragraph 1.

5. What countergeneralization is made in paragraph 3?

____

____

____

Paragraph 3 provides additional information that supports this countergeneralization.

6. What information supports this countergeneralization?

   a. ______________________________

   ____

   b. ______________________________

   ____

7. What conditions may be making the use of licensing agreements less effective for Japan?

   a. ______________________________

   ____

   b. ______________________________

   ____

DISCOURSE OUTLINE

Passage B follows the pattern of discourse below. Using the answers to questions 1–7, fill in the following outline.

Paragraph 1

1. Introduction: ______________________________

   ____

   ____

2. Example: ______________________________

   ____

3. Generalization: ______________________________

   ____

   ____

Paragraph 2

4. Development of Generalization with Examples:

   a. ______________________________

   ____

   b. ______________________________

   ____

Paragraph 2

c. ______________________________

____

d. ______________________________

____

e. ______________________________

____

Paragraph 3

5. Countergeneralization: ______________________________

____

____

6. Development of Countergeneralization with Examples:

a. ______________________________

____

b. ______________________________

7. Development of Countergeneralization with Examples:

a. ______________________________

____

b. ______________________________

____

Exercise 10

Look at the statements of *generalization* and *development* of generalization in Passage B. Write the main verb of these sentences in the blanks below.

1. ______________________ (l. 7)
2. ______________________ (l. 6)
3. What is the tense of these verbs?

____

Explanation: Statements of generalization and development of generalization are usually in the *present* tense.

Write the main verbs of the statements of *exemplification* in the blanks below.

4. ______________________ (l. 10)

5. ______________________ (l. 12)

6. ______________________ (ll. 13–14)

7. ______________________ (l. 16)

8. ______________________ (l. 19)

9. What are the tenses of these verbs?

____

Look at the statement of countergeneralization. Write the main verbs of these sentences in the blanks below.

10. ______________________ (l. 21)

11. ______________________ (l. 22)

12. ______________________ (l. 24)

13. Is the author certain that this countergeneralization is true?

____

14. How do you know this?

____

In the last two sentences of paragraph 3 the author presents information to support the countergeneralization. Write the main verbs of these statements in the blanks below.

15. ______________________ (l. 26)

16. ______________________ (l. 28)

17. What is the tense of these verbs?

____

18. Does the author believe that these statements are true?

____

19. How do you know this?

____

Exercise 11

Identify the function of each sentence in the paragraphs below. Then write the abbreviation for that function in the blank at the beginning of each sentence.

G = Generalization
DG = Development of Generalization
EX = Exemplification of Generalization
CG = Countergeneralization
DCG = Development of Countergeneralization

Paragraph A

_______ Modern science has discovered a great deal about people and their world. _______ It has improved lives in many important ways. _______ But it has also created dangers so great that there is risk to nearly every form of life. _______ Because of this risk, scientists must find new ways of controlling the effects of their discoveries so that they can make life safer for everyone. _______ The areas of atomic energy, biological science, and agriculture are especially important.

Paragraph B

_______ High school students who are planning to attend universities study many different subjects in school. _______ Each subject helps them to prepare for college in a different way. _______ The subjects they take include mathematics, chemistry, biology, foreign languages, and history.

Paragraph C

_______ Technology has improved people's condition in many areas. _______ It has affected health, transportation, education, employment, and business. _______ But the weapons that technology has created may eventually destroy the human race. _______ These weapons have become more powerful and more dangerous in recent years. _______ Long-range missiles, hydrogen bombs, and neutron bombs now represent serious threats to life on earth.

Paragraph D

_______ People who study foreign languages discover that there are many skills to be mastered. _______ These skills include listening, speaking, reading, and writing. _______ Some people believe that vocabulary development is the most important part of learning a foreign language. _______ For this reason, they use dictionaries a great deal. _______ However, recent research implies that listening and speaking may be more important for vocabulary learning than the use of dictionaries.

Exercise 12

Now answer these questions about paragraphs A through D in Exercise 11.

Paragraph A

1. What is one positive effect and one negative effect of modern science?

   a. ______________________________

   b. ______________________________

2. What must scientists do to correct the negative effects of science?

   a. ______________________________

   b. ______________________________

3. What three areas are particularly important?

   a. ______________________________

   b. ______________________________

   c. ______________________________

Paragraph B

4. Why do high school students who are planning to attend college study so many subjects?

   ____

   ____

5. What are three examples of these subjects?

   a. ______________________________

   b. ______________________________

   c. ______________________________

Paragraph C

6. What are three examples of areas in which technology has improved people's condition?

   a. ______

   b. ______

   c. ______

7. What may eventually destroy the human race?

   ______

8. What are three examples of weapons that could destroy life on earth?

   a. ______

   b. ______

   c. ______

Paragraph D

9. What are three examples of skills that must be mastered in learning a foreign language?

   a. ______

   b. ______

   c. ______

10. What do many people believe is the most important part of learning a foreign language?

    ______

11. What do these people study?

    ______

12. According to research, what may be more important for vocabulary development?

    ______

READING EXERCISE

Read the following passage and then do the exercises that follow.

According to the statistics which deal with American-controlled business, there are approximately 200 large American companies with overseas investments in manufacturing and raw materials. These business enterprises probably account for about one-third of the manufacturing within the United States itself. And through their branch offices they include about 6 to 8 percent of manufacturing sales in the other developed countries and 10 to 12 percent in the developing countries. In addition, there are many multinational enterprises with headquarters in other countries such as Britain, Germany, France, Italy, the Netherlands, Sweden, and Japan. Multinational enterprises add considerable amounts both to the national output of their home countries and to the foreign output of manufactured goods and raw materials.

Adapted from Raymond Vernon, 1971

Exercise 13

In each blank below, write the word from the Reading Exercise passage that has nearly the same meaning as the **boldface** word or phrase in the sentence.

1. Most multinational companies have **main offices** in their home countries.

   ____

2. **About** one-third of the manufacturing in the United States is done by multinational companies.

   ____

3. Many business decisions are based upon information that **is related to** economic conditions in various parts of the world.

   ____

4. Companies that conduct business **in foreign countries** frequently do so through the use of licensing agreements.

   ____

5. **Numerical information** about operational costs, output, and profit is essential for efficient planning of business enterprises.

   ____

6. Overseas manufacturing **explained** nearly one-fourth of the company's profits this year.

   ____

7. Multinational companies generally have **secondary** or **local** offices in many different countries.

   ____

Exercise 14

Answer the following questions, based on the Reading Exercise passage.

1. In what two areas of business do about 200 large American companies have overseas investments?

   ____

   ____

2. How much of the manufacturing sales in the United States do these enterprises account for?

   ____

3. What percentage of manufacturing sales in developing countries do such enterprises account for?

   ____

4. What are four countries in which multinational companies have headquarters?

   ____

   ____

   ____

   ____

5. To what two areas do multinational companies add considerably?

   ____

   ____

Lesson 10

Traditional Water Use Systems

PREREADING ACTIVITIES

A. Discussion Questions

1. What are some of the uses you make of water?
2. What are some of the different sources of the water you use?
3. Most of us can obtain water very easily by simply turning on a faucet. In many parts of the world, however, there are no modern water supply systems, and it is much more difficult to obtain water. If you lived in a place like this, where and how might you obtain your water?
4. Why might it be necessary to obtain water for different uses from different sources?

B. Special Vocabulary (Marked "*" in Passage A)

village	a group of houses, smaller than a town, in a rural area
ritual	a fixed procedure for conducting a special observance, often religious in nature
spring	a natural fountain or flow of water from out of the earth
puddle	a small amount of still water, naturally formed, on the ground

C. Guide Questions

As you read Passage A, ask yourself the following questions.

1. What are three reasons that people in isolated places obtain water from several different sources?
2. What two examples of water systems using more than one source are given?
3. In the valley in Mexico, what is the source of water used for washing clothes?
4. In Kuzistan, for what is water from a stream used?
5. Why can't people in Kuzistan use the spring water when it rains?
6. Why don't people in Kuzistan use water from puddles inside the village for drinking?

NOW READ PASSAGE A. WHEN YOU FINISH READING, ANSWER THE GUIDE QUESTIONS.

READING PASSAGES

Traditional Water Use Systems

Passage A

In small *villages and isolated areas, where **older customs and practices are followed,** the water which can be used is usually obtained from **more than one source.** Often, people need to get water from several **different** places because one source is not **enough** for all the needs of the village. In addition, there is less **danger** that the quality or the **amount** of water will **fail** if there are several different sources of water. Finally, getting water from more than one source **shows** the different values that are placed upon the quality, amount, and **ease** of access to water for the different purposes it serves.

For example, **look at the differences** in the ways water is used in Mexico and Iran. In an **isolated and faraway** valley in Mexico, drinking water comes from wells in the village. These wells are 3 to 10 meters deep. Water from these wells is also used for *ritual bathing, such as a mother's bathing after the birth of a child. A stream several kilometers away is used for ordinary bathing and for washing clothes. Each week, the washing of clothes is a social activity. The women of the **group** go to a specific place to wash clothes and to talk to their friends.

In Kuzistan, an area **out in the country** in Iran, water from a canal is used for washing pots and clothes. A special bathhouse by a stream outside the village is used for bathing. Water from a *spring about 50 kilometers away is used for drinking. This drinking water is brought by truck across the desert and people buy it by the gallon. When it rains, the road **cannot be used.** Therefore, people use rainwater for drinking. They obtain this rainwater from *puddles outside the village.

NOW GO BACK AND ANSWER THE GUIDE QUESTIONS.

Passage B

The main characteristic of **traditional** water use systems is that they are **multisource.** Often, **alternative** sources of water are necessary because one source is not **adequate** for all the needs of the **community.** In addition, the **risk** of **failure** in the quality or **quantity** of water is reduced by the presence of alternative sources. Finally, the use of more than one source **reflects** the different values which are placed upon the quality, quantity, and **convenience** of location for the various purposes it serves.

For example, **contrast** the water use systems in Mexico and Iran. In a **remote** valley in Mexico, drinking water is provided by wells 3 to 10 meters deep located within the village. Water from these wells is also used for ritual bathing, such as that of a mother after the birth of a child. However, a stream several kilometers away is used for ordinary bathing and for washing clothes. The weekly washing of clothes is a social activity. The women of the **community** go to a specific place to wash clothes and talk to their friends.

In Kuzistan, a **rural** area in Iran, water from a canal is used for washing pots and clothes. A special bathhouse located on a stream outside the village is used for bathing. Drinking water is provided by a spring about 50 kilometers away. The water is brought by truck across the desert and is bought by the gallon. Whenever it rains, the road is **unusable,** so drinking water is obtained from natural rainwater puddles outside the village.

COMPREHENSION EXERCISE

Exercise 1

Reread Passage B and then answer the questions below.

1. What is the main characteristic of traditional water use systems?

   ____

2. Why are several sources of water often necessary?

   a. ______________________________

   b. ______________________________

   c. ______________________________

3. In the remote valley in Mexico, what are four uses of water?

   a. ______________________________

   b. ______________________________

   c. ______________________________

   d. ______________________________

4. What sources provide water for these four uses?

   a. ____________ is used for ____________ and ____________

   b. ____________ is used for ____________ and ____________

5. What are three uses of water in Kuzistan?

   a. ______________________________

   b. ______________________________

   c. ______________________________

6. What sources provide water for these three uses?

   a. ____________ is used for ____________

   b. ____________ is used for ____________

   c. ____________ is used for ____________

7. What alternative source provides drinking water in Kuzistan?

   ____

8. When is this source used?

   ____

VOCABULARY EXERCISES

Exercise 2

Read each definition below and choose the word from the list that matches the definition. Then write that word in the blank.

adequate	convenience	risk
alternative	quantity	rural
community	reflect	tradition
contrast		

1. ______________________ to show
2. ______________________ a group of people living in the same area
3. ______________________ enough; sufficient
4. ______________________ to compare so that differences are made clear
5. ______________________ other (adj.); a choice between two things (n.)
6. ______________________ ease of use; suitability to one's needs
7. ______________________ amount or number of something
8. ______________________ older customs, beliefs, or practices
9. ______________________ possibility of danger or loss
10. ______________________ related to the country

Exercise 3

Fill in each blank with the correct word from the list. Each word is used only once.

adequate	convenience	risk
alternative	quantity	rural
community	reflects	traditional
contrast		

One characteristic of most ______________________ water use systems is that they are multisource. Often one source is not ______________________ because each ______________________ needs water for several different purposes. The presence of ______________________ sources reduces the ______________________ that the quality or ______________________ of water will fail. The use of different sources also ______________________ the different values placed upon the kind, amount, and ______________________ of the location of the water. An example of this is the ______________________ between the water use systems in ______________________ areas in Mexico and Iran.

WORD SKILLS

A. The noun suffix *-ure*

Examples from Passage B: fail*ure* (l. 4)

The suffix *-ure* is added to verbs to make nouns.

Examples: *Verb*	*Noun*	*Meaning*
enclose	enclosure*	something that is enclosed
erase	erasure*	something that is erased
depart	departure	the act of departing

*Note spelling change.

Exercise 4

Fill in the blanks below with the verb from which the underlined *-ure* noun is formed.

1. Maryam's family was sad because of her departure for England.

   Maryam's family was sad because she was ____________ for England.
2. John's failure on the test resulted in a low grade for the course.

   John's course grade was low because he ____________ the test.
3. Susan's enclosure of a small gift with the letter pleased her mother.

   Susan's mother was pleased that Susan had ____________ a small gift with the letter.

B. The adjective suffix *-ous*

Example from Passage B: vari*ous* (l. 7)

The suffix *-ous* is added to nouns to make adjectives. It means "possessing the quality of" or "related to."

Examples: *Noun*	*Adjective*
adventure	adventurous*
joy	joyous

*Note spelling change.

Exercise 5

In each blank below, write the noun from which the underlined *-ous* adjective is formed.

1. ____________________ The company moved into a spacious new office.
2. ____________________ There have been many accidents at that intersection; it's very dangerous.
3. ____________________ Professor Greenspan is a famous economist.
4. ____________________ The fall of the stock market was financially ruinous for many people.
5. ____________________ The courageous soldier saved his friend's life by a brave action.

DISCOURSE SKILLS

Exercise 6

Reread Passage B and then answer the questions below.

1. What generalization is made in the first paragraph?

____

____

2. What specific statements support this generalization?

a. ____

b. ____

c. ____

The second and third paragraphs of Passage B describe two situations that exemplify the generalization made in the first paragraph.

3. What two situations are examples of this generalization?

a. ____

____

b. ____

____

Exercise 7

Fill in the blanks below using information from Passage B.

Paragraph 1

1. Generalization:

____

____

2. Supporting statements:

a. ______________________________

____

b. ______________________________

____

c. ______________________________

____

Paragraph 2

3. Situation described:

____

4. Details of situation:

Water Source	Water Use
i. ______________	a. ______________ b. ______________
ii. ______________	c. ______________ d. ______________

Paragraph 3

5. Situation described:

____

6. Details of situation:

Water Source	Water Use
i. ______________	a. ______________
ii. ______________	b. ______________

iii. ____________________ c. ____________________

iv. ____________________ d. ____________________

Exercise 8

Go back and review Exercise 8, Lesson 7, on page 110, which deals with words and phrases that are used to signal examples. Then read the sentences below. In each sentence, do three things: (1) underline the generalization, (2) circle the word or phrase that signals the examples, and (3) put parentheses ( ) around each example.

Example: There are several ways for people who are studying a foreign language to improve their skills. (For instance,) they can (read magazines) and (listen to the radio.)

1. Governments can improve the health of young children in several ways that include providing clean water, building hospitals, and training doctors and nurses.
2. People who are learning about health care need to study many topics such as medicine, sanitation, food preparation, and disease control.
3. Numerous factors affect the health of people who live in isolated areas. For instance, clean water, good food, family planning, and adequate medical care are all important.
4. Education in literacy and training in health care, food production, and marketing are provided in many countries. Services such as these can help to improve the condition of women in poor areas.
5. The board conducts most of its business at an annual meeting. This includes the discussion of the annual financial report, the distribution of profits to shareholders, and the planning of new sales programs.

READING EXERCISE

Read the following passage and then do the exercises that follow.

The accessibility of clean water is one of the most important components in the health of young children. In many areas, disease caused by dirty water is a major cause of poor health and death among young children. This is a particular problem in rural areas, where sources of water may not be reliable, and neither the quantity nor the quality of the water is adequate.

In recent years, many programs to improve the quality of water supplies in rural areas have been implemented. These have included educating people about health and encouraging greater community involvement. In addition, many countries have improved the organization of government health control and technical services at both the national and local levels. Health control includes the establishment of regulations as well as close supervision and enforcement. Technical services, on the other hand, comprise a wide range of activities. These include providing supplies such as pumps, water pipes, and well-drilling equipment in addition to the training of people to operate and maintain this equipment. Technicians also help to organize the people of the community to build water supply projects. While access to pure water continues to be a problem in many parts of the world, programs such as these have contributed greatly to the general improvement of health in rural areas.

Exercise 9

In each blank below, write the word from the Reading Exercise passage that has nearly the same meaning as the **boldface** word or phrase in the sentence.

1. People in a community should be trained to **take care of** the equipment they use.

   ____

2. Technical services **consist of** both providing equipment and training people to operate and maintain that equipment.

   ____

3. Health education is an important **part** of any program to improve rural water supply systems.

   ____

4. A **dependable** water supply is essential to the health of a community.

   ____

5. The government will **put** its rural development plan **into effect** immediately.

   ____

6. In remote areas it is sometimes difficult to enforce **rules** dealing with food preparation and water supplies.

   ____

7. Many development programs provide training in **specialized** knowledge or skills.

   ____

8. **Making people obey** regulations is an important part of health control.

    ____

9. Several different factors **helped to bring about** the effectiveness of the program.

    ____

Exercise 10

Answer the following questions, based on the Reading Exercise passage.

1. What is a major cause of poor health and death in many areas?

    ____

2. Why is accessibility to clean water a particular problem in rural areas?

    ____

    ____

3. What have recent water improvement programs included?

    a. ____

    b. ____

4. What are three examples of technical services?

    a. ____

    b. ____

    c. ____

5. How successful have water improvement programs been?

    ____

Lesson 11

Reporting Crime in the Press

PREREADING ACTIVITIES

A. Discussion Questions

1. Do you think that what you believe about various topics is influenced by the way these topics are reported in the newspapers you read?
2. Do you think that different newspapers report news stories differently? If so, how do they differ?
3. What characteristics of newspapers determine what stories they report and how these stories are reported?
4. Find a news story that was reported by two different newspapers on the same day. In what ways are these two reports different?

B. Guide Questions
As you read Passage A, ask yourself the following questions.

1. Why were the two newspapers compared?
2. How many stories were compared?
3. What three factors were examined?
4. How much space did each newspaper give to reporting details of the crime itself?
5. On which factor were the differences between the two newspapers the greatest?
6. Why is it important to conduct other studies like this one?

NOW READ PASSAGE A. WHEN YOU FINISH READING, ANSWER THE GUIDE QUESTIONS.

READING PASSAGES

Reporting Crime in the Press

Adapted from John C. Meyer, Jr., 1976

Passage A

Many people believe that society's **idea** of crime is based on the way it is reported in newspapers. To examine whether there are differences **in the amount** of space that newspapers use to report crime stories, the New York *Times* and the New York *Daily News* were chosen for study. These newspapers were chosen because they had been cited as **not agreeing** in their styles of reporting crime. Thirty-seven stories which reported crime were selected **by chance** and the content **examined closely.** In all, 74 stories (that is, one report from each newspaper for each crime story reported on the same day) were examined closely by **counting** each piece of information that dealt with three factors: the crime, the offender, and any actions taken by **government officials** in the processing of the case.

An examination of the **information** from the comparison on these three factors showed that there were few differences between the two newspapers. Each newspaper **gave** nearly half of the total amount of information per story to reporting the details of the crime itself. The *News* gave **slightly more** (51 percent) than the *Times* (49 percent), but this difference does not approach practical or **numerical** significance. In reporting information about the offender, the *News* gave 17 percent of its space, compared to the *Times*' 15 percent, a difference that again is not large enough to be significant.

However, the **examination of the results** of the study showed that the *Times* gave a larger **part** of its stories (22 percent) to the official actions of the **representatives** of the criminal justice system than did the *News* (16 percent). This difference is not large, but it is greater than those found for the other two factors. It would appear then, that the New York *Times* reports more of the actions of the criminal justice **offices and representatives** than does the New York *Daily News.*

While we are **not entirely certain** of these results, we could perhaps conclude that newspapers that are considered "conservative," such as the New York *Times,* may tend to report more of what happens after the **committing** of a crime, when that crime **is worth** reporting in the newspaper. Although other **studies** like this one ought to be **conducted in the same way** to **determine if** these results are **correct,** it may be productive for now to consider that the public's idea of the criminal justice process may be influenced by newspapers.

Passage B

Many people believe that society's **conception** of crime is based on the way it is reported in newspapers. To examine whether there are **quantitative** differences in the crime reporting styles of newspapers, two newspapers, the New York *Times* and the New York *Daily News,* were chosen for study. These newspapers were chosen because they had been cited as **disagreeing** in their styles of reporting crime. Thirty-seven crime stories were **randomly** selected and their content **analyzed.** In all, 74 stories (that is, each paper's reporting of the same crime when stories were published on the same day) were analyzed by **enumerating** each piece of information that dealt with three factors: the crime, the offender, and any actions taken by **authorities** in the processing of the case.

An examination of the **data** for these three elements showed there to be few quantitative differences between the two newspapers. Each newspaper **devoted** nearly half of the total amount of information per story to reporting the details of the crime itself. The *News* had a **slight edge** (51 percent) over the *Times* (49 percent), but this difference does not approach practical or **statistical** significance. In reporting information about the offender, the *News* devoted 17 percent of its space, in comparison to the *Times*' 15 percent, a difference that again is not large enough to be significant.

However, the **analysis** showed that the *Times* devoted a larger **proportion** of information (22 percent) to the official actions of the criminal justice system's **agents** than did the *News* (16 percent). While this difference in totals is not large, it is greater than those found for the other two factors. It would appear then, that the New York *Times* reports more of the actions of the criminal justice **agencies** than does the New York *Daily News*.

It may **tentatively** be concluded that newspapers that are considered "conservative," such as the New York *Times,* may tend to report more of what happens after the **commission** of a crime, when that crime **merits** reporting in the newspaper. Although this **research** ought to be **replicated** to **verify** these results, it may be productive for now to consider that the public's conception of the criminal justice process may be influenced by newspapers.

COMPREHENSION EXERCISE

Exercise 1

Reread Passage B and then answer the questions below.

In the first paragraph, the author states his reason for making the comparison.

1. What is the purpose of the comparison?

    ____

2. What two newspapers were compared?

    ____

    ____

3. Why were these two newspapers chosen?

    ____

    ____

4. How were the crime stories selected?

    ____

5. How were the stories analyzed?

    ____

6. What specific factors of the crime stories are compared?

    ____

    ____

    ____

In the second paragraph, the author states the results of the comparison. The first sentence states what the results were in *general*.

7. In general, what did the comparison show?

    ____

In the rest of the paragraph, the author states *specifically* what the results of the comparison were.

8. What did the results show about the first factor?

    ____

    ____

9. Exactly what proportion of information did the *Daily News* devote to this factor?

    ____

10. What proportion did the *Times* devote to this factor?

    ____

11. Is this difference in percentages significant?

    ____

12. What was the second factor studied?

    ____

13. What proportion did the *News* devote to this factor?

____

14. What proportion did the *Times* devote to this factor?

____

15. Is this difference significant?

____

16. What was the third factor in the comparison?

____

17. What proportion did the *News* devote to this factor?

____

18. What proportion did the *Times* devote to this factor?

____

19. Is this difference larger or smaller than the differences for the other two factors?

____

VOCABULARY EXERCISES

Exercise 2

In each blank below, write the word from the list that best matches the definition.

agent	enumerate	replicate
analyze	merit	research
conception	proportion	tentative
data	random	verify

1. _______________ an idea or thought
2. _______________ to test the truth of something
3. _______________ representative
4. _______________ to earn or deserve worth
5. _______________ by chance; without pattern or objective
6. _______________ not completely accepted or proven

7. ____________________ the relationship between a part and a whole
8. ____________________ to count
9. ____________________ to examine something in terms of its parts
10. ____________________ to repeat or copy
11. ____________________ scientific investigation
12. ____________________ information organized for analysis

Exercise 3

Fill in each blank below with a word from the list. Each word is used only once.

agents	enumerating	replicated
analyzed	merits	research
conception	proportion	tentative
data	randomly	verify

Many people believe that the way society thinks of crime is influenced by the ____________________ of crime as it is reported in newspapers. To study this, ____________________ was conducted in which crime stories from two newspapers were ____________________ selected and their content ____________________ by ____________________ each piece of information. The newspapers were chosen because they had been cited as disagreeing in their crime reporting styles.

Although the ____________________ from the study showed that in general there were few quantitative differences between the two newspapers, the *Times* did devote a larger ____________________ of information to the official actions of the criminal justice system's ____________________ than the *News*. To ____________________ these results, this study should be ____________________.

Nevertheless, one ____________________ conclusion may be that "conservative" newspapers tend to report more of what happens after a crime is committed than of details of the crime itself, when the crime ____________________ reporting in the newspaper.

WORD SKILLS

The prefix *dis-*

Example from Passage B: *dis*agreeing (l. 5)

The prefix *dis-* forms negatives of the words to which it is added. It is added to verbs, nouns, and sometimes adjectives.

Examples: *Word*	*Meaning*
disadvantage	not a help
discontinue	to stop; not to continue

Exercise 4

Add the prefix *dis-* to the following words and then write the new words in the correct blanks below.

appear	honest	prove
connect	organize	

1. Ancient theories about the nature of matter have been ________________________ by modern scientific research.
2. Storms can sometimes cause telephone lines to be ________________________.
3. The employee was not promoted because he was very ________________________.
4. The sun appears in the morning and ________________________ at night.
5. No one likes a person who seldom tells the truth and who is ________________________.

DISCOURSE SKILLS

Exercise 5

Fill in the blanks below using information from Passage B. First write the factors that were compared. Then write the percentage that each newspaper devoted to that factor. Next, write the name of the newspaper that devoted the larger percentage to that factor. Finally, write the differences in the percentages between the two newspapers.

	Factor Compared	Percentages in News	Percentages in Times	Paper with Larger Percentage	Difference
1.	________				
	________	______	______	______	______
2.	________				
	________	______	______	______	______
3.	________				
	________				
	________				
	________	______	______	______	______

Exercise 6

Below is a chart of the comparisons made in Passage B. Fill in the blanks with information from the passage.

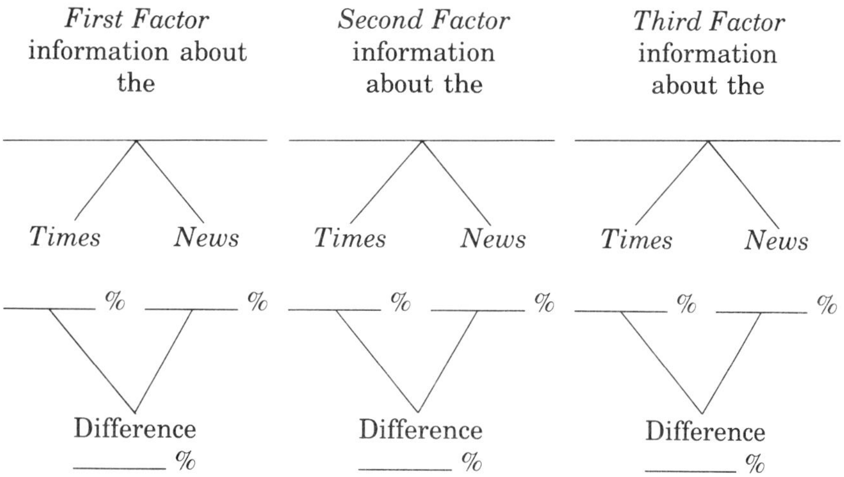

Exercise 7

Comparative Constructions

A *comparative construction* contains two elements that are compared according to some characteristic they have in common. The comparison is often indicated by comparative markers such as *-er, more, less,* or *worse,* together with the word *than.*

Examples:

The Times has *more* readers *than* *the News* does.

Element 1 — *The Times*; Comparative Marker — *more*; Element 2 — *the News*

Magazines devote *more* space to *international news than* to *local news.*

Comparative Marker — *more*; Element 1 — *international news*; Element 2 — *local news*

The sentences below all contain comparative constructions. In each sentence, underline the two elements of the comparison and circle the comparative markers.

1. The analysis showed that the *Times* devoted a larger proportion of information to the official actions of the criminal justice system's agents than did the *News*.
2. It would appear that the New York *Times* reports more of the actions of the criminal justice agencies than does the New York *Daily News*.
3. In reporting information about the offender, the *News* devoted more of its space than the *Times*.
4. Both newspapers devoted more space to information dealing with the crime itself than to information dealing with the offender.
5. The difference in percentages of information dealing with the official actions of the criminal justice system's agents is greater than the differences found for the other two factors.

Exercise 8

Comparison phrases *few, a few, little, a little*

***Few, a few, little,* and *a little* all mean "small amounts." *Few* and *little,* when used as comparison phrases, are negative. *A few* and *a little,* however, are neutral.**

Examples: He has *few* [not many] friends and *little* [not much] money.
He has *a few* [some] friends and *a little* [some] money.

An author uses phrases like *few differences* or *little difference* in a comparative construction to emphasize, or give more importance to, discussing the ways in which the elements of the comparison are the **same.** An author uses phrases like *a few differences* or *a little difference* in a comparative construction to emphasize the ways in which the two elements are **different.**

Read the paragraphs below and then answer the questions that follow.

Paragraph A

There are few differences between the two cultures. The languages that are spoken in the two countries are almost the same. In both countries the major religion is Islam. One country has more industry than the other, but people from each country still believe in the importance of the family.

1. Does the author want to emphasize that the two cultures are similar or different? ____________________
2. In what elements are the countries similar? ____________________, ____________________, ____________________
3. How are they different? ____________________

Paragraph B

There were a few changes in his appearance since I had last seen him. He was taller than when I saw him a year ago. His hair was longer too, and the clothes he wore were more stylish and fashionable. But he still spoke quietly and had a warm smile.

4. Does the author want to emphasize that the person's appearance had changed or remained the same? ____________________
5. How has the person's appearance changed? ____________________, ____________________, ____________________
6. How has he remained the same? ____________________, ____________________

Paragraph C

There is little difference in the two magazines. Both are published once a week, and both report the latest news events. They often have similar photographs on the front page. One magazine is larger than the other, but this difference is not important.

7. Does the author mean to emphasize that the magazines are similar or different? ______________________

8. How are the magazines similar? ______________________, ______________________, ______________________

9. How are they different? ______________________

READING EXERCISE

Read the following passage and then do the exercises that follow.

In addition to newspapers and periodical journals, there are two other media which are important to criminal investigators. They are radio and television, and for the investigator they represent a very useful means of obtaining the assistance of the public.

Of the two, television is the more valuable because of the large amount of time it devotes to reporting crime stories. Also, on television, it is possible to show pictures of persons whom the investigator wishes to interview rather than rely only on verbal descriptions. Such descriptions may help the trained investigator as a means of identification, but they are unlikely to help members of the public to recognize anyone unless he or she has some outstanding physical features. One aspect of radio, however, makes it more valuable than television in immediately alerting the public to be on the lookout for persons whom the investigator wishes to contact. This is the fact that there are more radios in use, not only in homes, but also in automobiles and outdoors. Consequently, more people can be reached at all hours of the day than can be reached by television.

Written by Edward Weidhmann, 1977

Exercise 9

In each blank below, write the word from the Reading Exercise passage that has nearly the same meaning as the **boldface** word or phrase in the sentence.

1. Newspapers, magazines, and movies are examples of **means of communicating with large numbers of people.**

   ____

2. The company is **not expected** to reach its goal of a 10 percent increase in production this year.

   ____

3. Investigators **depend** upon many sources of information in solving a crime.

   ____

4. Most businesspersons regularly read a professional **newspaper or magazine** in their special area of expertise.

   ____

5. Pictures of the criminal were broadcast over television, and **as a result,** several people were able to identify him.

   ____

6. One particularly valuable **characteristic** of the media is its capability for performing public services.

   ____

7. Modern plants have equipment for **warning** workers of any danger that might arise.

   ____

8. The reporter provided a detailed description **in words** of the person being sought by investigators.

   ____

9. The salesperson's excellent performance last month was **very noticeable.**

   ____

Exercise 10

Answer the following questions, based on the Reading Exercise passage.

1. What four media are important to criminal investigators?

   ____

   ____

   ____

   ____

2. In what ways is television more valuable than radio?

   ____

   ____

3. Who is most likely to be helped by verbal descriptions?

   ____

4. In what ways is radio more valuable to the investigator than television?

____

____

5. Why is this so?

____

Lesson 12

Japanese and American Attitudes toward the Abolition of Capital Punishment

PREREADING ACTIVITIES

A. Discussion Questions

1. Do you know what capital punishment is? How would you define it?
2. How do you feel about capital punishment?
3. Do you think other people feel the same way?
4. How might a person's age, level of education, and culture affect how he or she feels about capital punishment?
5. Find out how many of your classmates agree or disagree with capital punishment. What are their reasons for feeling the way they do?

B. Special Vocabulary (Marked "*" in Passage A)

capital punishment	executing people for the commission of certain crimes
homicide	murder
kidnap	to carry away a person by force
arson	the crime of intentionally setting something on fire

C. Guide Questions

As you read Passage A, ask yourself the following questions.

1. What crimes are sometimes punished by the death penalty?
2. What two national groups were studied?
3. For which nationality does the smaller percentage of persons want to end capital punishment?
4. For what two groups in both nationalities does the largest percentage want to end capital punishment?
5. For what age group is there the largest difference between Americans and Japanese?
6. At what educational level are Americans and Japanese most similar?
7. In general, what type of American is most likely to want to end capital punishment?
8. Is this the same for Japanese? Why or why not?

NOW READ PASSAGE A. WHEN YOU FINISH READING, ANSWER THE GUIDE QUESTIONS.

READING PASSAGES

Japanese and American Attitudes toward the Abolition of Capital Punishment

Adapted from Jon P. Alston, 1976

Passage A

The question of **putting an end to** *capital punishment is one about which there is disagreement **in many places.** People in the same country disagree about this question, as do people in different countries. In most cases, capital punishment applies to crimes resulting in *homicide. **There are a few cases where this is not so,** where **execution** applies to other crimes, such as *kidnapping in America or *arson in Japan. The **argument** about capital punishment, however, usually involves homicides of one kind or another. To examine differences in the **way people** in different countries **feel** about ending capital punishment, a **scientific investigation** of Americans and Japanese was recently conducted. According to the results of this study, most Americans and Japanese do not **want** to put an end to capital punishment.

This research also indicates that fewer Japanese than Americans want to put an end to capital punishment. **Groups chosen to represent** Americans and Japanese were asked the question, "Do you **agree with** the execution of persons **found guilty** of committing murder?" Table 1 on page 178 presents some of the data obtained in **answer** to this question. Thirty-nine percent of the Americans who answered wanted to put an end to capital punishment, while 53 percent did not. Similarly, 16 percent of all the Japanese who answered wanted to put an end to capital punishment, though 71 percent did not. This difference among the Japanese was larger than that found among the Americans. Of the Americans, more females wanted to end capital punishment (41 percent) than did males (29 percent). Of the Japanese, more males wanted to end capital punishment (17 percent) than did females (15 percent).

Table 2 on page 179 **gives more** data about the **part of the group** of Americans and Japanese who agreed with ending capital punishment for persons found guilty of murder. Forty-six percent of the Americans who were under 30 years of age wanted to end capital punishment. However, only 30 percent of those of 50 years and older did. **In the same way,** 23 percent of the Japanese under 30 wanted to end capital punishment, but only 11 percent of those of 50 and older did. Of the Americans who answered, **although** only 34 percent of those who had a primary school education wanted to end capital punishment, 37 percent of those who had a college education did. Similarly, only 12 percent of the Japanese who had a primary school education wanted to end capital punishment, while 29 percent of those who had a college education did.

The data from this research **show** some ways in which Americans and Japanese are similar in the way they feel about ending capital punishment. The results also show some ways in which these two groups are different in their feelings. In both groups more people who were under 30 wanted to end capital punishment than did people who were 50 and older. In the same way, more people who had a college education wanted to end capital punishment than did those who had only a primary school education. The two groups were different, however, **in relation to** sex. More American females than males wanted to end capital punishment, while among Japanese, more males than females wanted to end capital punishment. Finally, a much much smaller percentage of Japanese than Americans wanted to end capital punishment.

Passage B

The **abolition** of capital punishment is an issue about which there is **widespread** disagreement, not only among people in a given country, but also among different nationalities. Although **exceptions exist,** such as the **death penalty** for kidnapping in America or for arson in Japan, the **controversy** over capital punishment usually involves homicides of one form or another. To investigate differences in **attitudes** toward the abolition of capital punishment among different nationalities, a **survey** of Americans and Japanese was conducted. According to the results of this study, the majority of Americans and Japanese do not **favor** the abolition of capital punishment for homicide.

The research also indicates that Japanese favor the abolition of capital punishment less than Americans. **Samples** of Americans and Japanese were asked the question, "Are you **in favor of** the death penalty for persons **convicted** of murder?" Table 1 following presents some of the data obtained in **response** to this question. Thirty-nine percent of the American sample favored abolition, while 53 percent did not. A similar, but larger difference was observed in the Japanese sample, while 16 percent favored abolition, though 71 percent did not. In the American sample more females favored abolition (41 percent) than did males (29 percent), while in the Japanese sample more males (17 percent) than females (15 percent) favored abolition.

Table 2 on page 179 below **supplies additional** data about the **subsample** of Americans and Japanese who favored the abolition of capital punishment for persons convicted of murder. Forty-six percent of the American sample under 30 years of age favored abolition, while only 30 percent of those of 50 years and older did. **Likewise,** 23 percent of the Japanese under 30 favored abolition, but only 11 percent of those of 50 and older did. In the American sample, only 34 percent of those with a primary school education favored abolition, **whereas** 37 percent of those with a college education did. Similarly, only 12 percent of the Japanese with a primary school education favored abolition, while 29 percent of those with a college education did.

The data from this research **reveal** both similarities and differences between American and Japanese attitudes toward the abolition of capital punishment. In both samples, more people under 30 years of age were in favor of abolition than were people of 50 and older. Similarly, more people with a college education favored abolition than did those with only a primary school education. However, a difference between the two samples **with regard to** sex was observed. More American females than males favored abolition, whereas in the Japanese sample, more males than females favored abolition. Finally, although in both samples fewer people favored abolition than did not, the percentage of people in favor of abolition was much smaller in the Japanese sample than in the American.

Table 1 Attitudes Toward the Abolition of Capital Punishment in America and Japan, by Sex

	% IN FAVOR OF ABOLITION	*% NOT IN FAVOR OF ABOLITION*	*% WHO DO NOT KNOW*
American males	29	67	4
American females	41	48	11
Japanese males	17	74	9
Japanese females	15	67	18
Total Americans	39	53	8
Total Japanese	16	71	13

Table 2 Percentage in Favor of Abolishing Capital Punishment, by Nationality, Age, and Level of Education

AGE AND EDUCATION	% AMERICAN	% JAPANESE
Age		
Under 30	46	23
30–39	36	16
40–49	30	16
50 and older	30	11
Highest level of education		
Primary school	34	12
High school	34	18
College	37	29

COMPREHENSION EXERCISES

Exercise 1

Reread Passage B and then answer the questions below.

1. The main idea of the passage is given in the first paragraph. What is the main idea of the passage?

   ____

   ____

2. What general finding is given in the first paragraph?

   ____

   ____

3. What two generalizations can be made from the findings given in the second paragraph?

   a. ______________________________

   ____

   b. ______________________________

   ____

4. What generalizations can be made from the findings given in the third paragraph?

   a. ______________________________

   ____

   b. ______________________________

   ____

5. According to the last paragraph, how are Americans and Japanese similar in their attitudes toward capital punishment?

   a. ____

   ____

   b. ____

   ____

6. How are they different?

   ____

   ____

7. What tentative conclusion does the author draw from this research?

   ____

   ____

Exercise 2

An author will sometimes omit a word or phrase from a sentence if that word or phrase has been mentioned before. This is done to avoid repetition.

> Example: For both Americans and Japanese, more people with a college education were in favor of abolition than people with a high school education were in favor of abolition.

In this sentence, the phrase "in favor of abolition" is repeated, and the sentence is awkward. To avoid this repetition, the repeated phrase could be omitted, and the sentence rewritten as follows:

> For both Americans and Japanese, more people with a college education were in favor of abolition than were people with a high school education.

1. In the following sentence from Passage B, what phrase has been omitted?

   This research also indicated that Japanese favor the abolition of capital punishment less than Americans.

   ____

2. What phrase has been omitted from the following sentence?

   In both samples, more people under 30 years of age were in favor of abolition than were people of 50 and older.

   ____

Sometimes an author will use a form of the verb "do" rather than repeat an entire phrase.

Example: In the American sample, more females favored abolition than *did* males.

In this sentence, the word "did" indicates that the phrase "favored abolition" has been omitted to avoid repetition.

Answer the following questions by referring back to Passage B.

3. In line 17, what omitted phrase does *did not* represent?

____

4. In line 27, what omitted phrase does *did* represent?

____

5. In line 34, what omitted phrase does *did* represent?

____

6. In line 38, what omitted phrase does *did not* represent?

____

VOCABULARY EXERCISES

Exercise 3

In each blank below, write the word from the list that best matches the definition.

abolition	exception	survey
attitude	response	widespread
controversy	reveal	whereas
convict	sample	

1. ____________ the act of putting an end to something
2. ____________ an answer
3. ____________ a lengthy and public argument
4. ____________ found over a large area
5. ____________ to find or prove guilty in a court of law
6. ____________ a part or group that represents a whole
7. ____________ but; in contrast; although

8. ______________________ a case that does not follow a rule or generalization
9. ______________________ to show; to make known
10. ______________________ a way of feeling, thinking or behaving
11. ______________________ a detailed inspection

Exercise 4

Fill in each blank below with the correct word from the list. Each word is used only once.

abolition	exceptions	survey
attitudes	responses	widespread
controversy	revealed	whereas
convicted	samples	

The ______________________ over capital punishment is ______________________, and although there are ______________________, this debate usually involves its use in cases of homicide. While the majority of Americans and Japanese support capital punishment, a larger percentage of Americans favor its ______________________ than do Japanese. These conclusions are suggested by data from a ______________________ involving ______________________ of Americans and Japanese. Data were obtained from ______________________ to the question, "Do you favor the death penalty for persons ______________________ of murder?" Analysis of the answers to this question ______________________ that American and Japanese ______________________ toward capital punishment are similar with regard to age, ______________________ they are different with respect to sex.

WORD SKILLS

The prefix *sub-*

Example from Passage B: *sub*sample (l. 21)

The prefix *sub-* is added to nouns, adjectives, and verbs. It has the meaning "under," "lower than," "lesser in rank," or "part of."

Examples: *Word*	*Meaning*
subdivide	to divide into smaller parts
subhuman	less than human
subcommittee	a lower committee, part of a larger committee

Exercise 5

Add the prefix *sub-* to each of the following words and then write each word in the appropriate blank below.

urban	way
division	title
total	

1. We rode underneath the streets, on the ____________________ on our way to work.
2. The ____________________ of this book is very long, so I wrote down only the title.
3. We need to total our expenses for the entire year. Could you please give me the ____________________ for each month, as well?
4. The housing committee has divided the area into several ____________________.
5. We live at the edge of the city, in a ____________________ area.

DISCOURSE SKILLS

Exercise 6

Answer the following questions, based on Passage B.

1. Table 1 compares the responses of six groups of people. What are these six groups?

____

____

____

____

____

____

2. What two groups had the smallest percentages of responses in favor of abolition?

____

____

3. What characteristic do these two groups have in common?

____

4. What characteristic is shared by the two groups with 15 percent and 41 percent in favor of abolition?

____

In a comparative construction two elements are compared with respect to a common characteristic that is the *criterion* of the comparison.

Each of the characteristics in 1–4 can be used as a basis or *criterion* for comparison. Using these characteristics as *criteria* for comparisons, answer the following questions.

5. With respect to nationality, are more Americans or Japanese in favor of abolition?

____

6. With respect to sex, are more females or males in favor of abolition?

____

Exercise 7

Answer the following questions, based on Passage B.

1. In Table 2 on page 179 the responses of people are compared with respect to two criteria. What are these two criteria?

____

____

2. What four groups are compared with respect to the first criterion?

____

____

____

____

3. What three groups are compared with respect to the second criterion?

____

____

____

4. The responses are also compared with respect to the criterion of nationality. What two groups are compared with respect to this criterion?

____

____

5. What age group of Americans has the highest percentage in Table 2?

______________________ (______ percent)

6. Does the same age group of Japanese have the highest percentage?

____

7. What age group of Japanese has the lowest percentage in Table 2?

______________________ (______ percent)

8. Does the same age group of Americans have the lowest percentage?

____

9. What generalization in paragraph 4 is based on these responses?

____

____

10. For Americans, what group, with respect to education, has the highest percentage in Table 2?

____

11. For Americans, what group, with respect to education, has the lowest percentage?

____

12. Do the same groups of Japanese have the highest and lowest percentages?

____

13. What generalization in paragraph 4 is based on these responses?

____

____

Exercise 8

In each sentence below, underline the two elements of the comparison, circle the comparative marker, and put *two* lines under the criterion of the comparison.

Example:	Fewer	American males	than	females
	Comparative Marker	Element 1		Element 2

favor the abolition of capital punishment.

Criterion

1. Japanese favor the abolition of capital punishment less than Americans.
2. In the Japanese sample more males than females favored abolition.
3. More people under 30 years of age were in favor of abolition than were people 50 and older.
4. In the Japanese sample, the percentage of people in favor of abolition was much larger for people with a college education than for those with only a primary school education.
5. The *Times* devotes a larger proportion of information to the official actions of the criminal justice systems' agents than does the *Daily News*.
6. Both newspapers devote more space to information dealing with the crime itself than to information dealing with the offender.
7. Generally speaking, skilled labor tends to be more specific than unskilled labor.
8. Stocks are a better investment when the economy is growing than when economic conditions are not good.
9. People's living conditions have changed more rapidly in the past 200 years than in the thousands of years that preceded.
10. By 1958, French life had become much more industrialized and urbanized than it had ever been before.

Exercise 9

A contrastive construction is similar to a comparative construction, since it also contains two elements, or sets of information. A contrastive construction, however, emphasizes how these two elements are *different* with respect to the criterion of the contrast.

In Passage B six words mark contrastive constructions. These words are

although	though
but	whereas
however	while

In each of the sentences below, circle the contrastive marker, and then write in the blanks the two contrasting elements and the criterion upon which they differ.

Example: Thirty-nine percent of the American sample favored abolition, whereas only 16 percent of the Japanese sample did.

Element 1: american sample

Element 2: Japanese sample

Criterion: percentage favoring abolition

1. Thirty-nine percent of the American sample favored abolition, while 53 percent did not.

   Element 1: ______

   Element 2: ______

   Criterion: ______

2. A similar, but larger, difference was observed in the Japanese sample, where 16 percent favored abolition, though 71 percent did not.

   Element 1: ______

   Element 2: ______

   Criterion: ______

3. Forty-six percent of the American sample under 30 years of age favored abolition, while only 30 percent of those of 50 and older did.

   Element 1: ______

   Element 2: ______

   Criterion: ______

4. Likewise, 25 percent of the Japanese under 30 favored abolition, but only 11 percent of those of 50 and older did.

   Element 1: ______________________________

   Element 2: ______________________________

   Criterion: ______________________________

5. In the American sample, whereas only 34 percent of those with only a primary school education favored abolition, 37 percent of those with a college education did.

   Element 1: ______________________________

   Element 2: ______________________________

   Criterion: ______________________________

6. Similarly, only 12 percent of the Japanese with only primary school education favored abolition, while 29 percent of those with a college education did.

   Element 1: ______________________________

   Element 2: ______________________________

   Criterion: ______________________________

7. More American females than males favored abolition, whereas in the Japanese sample, more males than females favored abolition.

   Element 1: ______________________________

   Element 2: ______________________________

   Criterion: ______________________________

   ____

8. Although exceptions exist, such as the death penalty for kidnapping in America or for arson in Japan, the controversy over capital punishment usually involves homicides of one form or another.

   Element 1: ______________________________

   Element 2: ______________________________

   Criterion: ______________________________

9. Table 1 presents data about both people who favor and people who do not favor the abolition of capital punishment, while Table 2 presents data only about people who favor the abolition of capital punishment.

   Element 1: ______________________________

   Element 2: ______________________________

   Criterion: ______________________________

10. Although in both samples fewer people favored abolition than did not, the percentage of people in favor of abolition was much smaller in the Japanese sample than in the American.

    Element 1: ______________________________

    ____

    Element 2: ______________________________

    ____

    Criterion: ______________________________

    ____

11. The data from these samples reveal both similarities and differences between American and Japanese attitudes toward the abolition of capital punishment. In both samples more people under 30 years of age were in favor of abolition than were people of 50 and older. Similarly, more people with a college education favored abolition than did those with a primary school education. However, there was a difference between the two samples with regard to sex.

    Element 1: ______________________________

    ____

    Element 2: ______________________________

    ____

    Criterion: ______________________________

    ____

READING EXERCISE

Read the following passage and then do the exercises that follow.

Several recent studies indicate that compared with females, males commit a great excess of crimes in all nations, all communities within nations, all age groups, all periods of history for which we have statistics, and nearly all types of crime. The sex ratio for arrested criminals varies with place, time, and age. One study has indicated a criminal sex ratio of 350 males per 100 females for Belgium compared with a ratio of approximately 3,000 to 1 in Algiers and Tunis. It was concluded that the criminal sex ratios are highest in societies where females are rigidly supervised and lowest in societies in which females have the greatest freedom and the closest approximation to equality with males.

The criminal sex ratio is lower in American cities than in small towns, probably reflecting the differences in the amount of freedom permitted in the two types of communities. In large cities, the ratio is lowest in high-crime areas and highest in low-crime areas. There is evidence that the criminal sex ratio has been decreasing, especially in recent years, as women have acquired statuses more nearly equal to those of men.

Adapted from L. Broom and P. Selznick, 1968.

Exercise 10

In each blank below, write the word from the Reading Exercise passage that has nearly the same meaning as the **boldface** word or phrase.

1. Crime rates tend to be lower in those countries where the laws are **firmly** enforced.

   ____

2. In Belgium, the **proportion** of male to female criminals is much lower than in Algiers or Tunis.

   ____

3. After a search of many weeks, the police were finally able to **seize and hold** the suspected criminal.

   ____

4. The criminal sex ratio **is different** in American cities and small towns.

   ____

5. The researchers found **data** to support their idea that males commit more crimes than females.

   ____

6. In highly technical industries, it is necessary to **direct** workers very carefully.

   ____

7. Several studies indicate that in comparison to females, males commit an **extra amount** of crimes all over the world.

   ____

8. In recent years, the **social and professional position** of women has become more nearly equal to that of men.

   ____

Exercise 11

Answer the following questions, based on the Reading Exercise passage.

1. What generalization does the author make on the basis of several recent studies?

   ____

2. In what kind of societies is the proportion of male criminals the lowest?

   ____

   ____

3. Is the proportion of female criminals lower in American cities or in American small towns?

   ____

4. According to the author, why is this the case?

   ____

   ____

5. Has the ratio of male to female criminals been increasing or decreasing?

   ____

6. Why does the author believe this has happened?

   ____

   ____

Lesson 13

Social Change

PREREADING ACTIVITIES

A. Discussion Questions

1. What kinds of changes might be called social changes? Give some examples of social changes.
2. What social changes have taken place in your country in the past 100 years?
3. What social changes have taken place during your lifetime?
4. Have similar changes happened during this time in other countries?
5. Do you think that social change occurs more quickly in some countries or time periods than in others?
6. In what kinds of societies is social change most likely to occur?
7. What factors determine the ease or speed with which social change occurs?

B. Special Vocabulary (Marked "*" in Passage A)

dichotomy   division into two separate parts or groups

C. Guide Questions
As you read Passage A, ask yourself the following questions.

1. In what kind of society is social change most likely to occur?
2. What factors tend to promote social change?

3. Does disagreeing with or arguing about conditions tend to promote or to slow down social change?
4. In which aspect of society is social change more likely to occur, the material or the nonmaterial?
5. Does change occur more easily in matters like religion or in technical matters?
6. Has social change come more quickly to Black Americans or to other social groups?

NOW READ PASSAGE A. WHEN YOU FINISH READING, ANSWER THE GUIDE QUESTIONS.

READING PASSAGES

Social Change

Adapted from Bernard Berelson and Gary A. Steiner, 1967

Passage A

Social change is more likely to occur in societies where there is a **mixture of different kinds** of people than in societies where people are **similar in many ways.** The **simple** reason for this is that there are more **different ways of looking at things present** in **the first** kind of society. There are more ideas, more **disagreements** in interest, and more groups and organizations with different **beliefs.** In addition, there is usually a greater worldly interest and greater **respect for the beliefs and behavior of others** in mixed societies. All these factors tend to promote social change by opening more areas of life to decision rather than **keeping** them **under the control** of authority. In a society where people are quite similar in many ways, there are fewer occasions for people to **see** the need or the opportunity for change because everything seems to be the same. And although conditions may not be satisfactory, they are at least customary, and no one **disagrees with or argues about** them.

Within a society, social change is also likely to occur more frequently and more **easily** (1) in the material aspects of culture than in the nonmaterial, for example, in technology rather than in **standards of behavior and belief;** (2) in the things people have learned later in life rather than what they learned when they were young; and (3) in the less basic, less emotional, and less **holy** aspects rather than their opposites, like religion or a system of **social importance.** Change is also more common (4) in the simple elements rather than the complex ones, (5) in form rather than in **content,** and (6) in the elements that are **acceptable** to the culture rather than in strange elements.

Furthermore, social change is easier if it is gradual. For example, change happens more easily in human relations on a scale where **differences are small and gradual** rather than on one with **clear** *dichotomies. This is one reason why change has not come more quickly to Black Americans, as compared with other **social groups which are small in number.** This is because of the great difference in appearance between them and Americans who are **similar** to them **in most characteristics,** but who are white.

Passage B

Social change is more likely to occur in **heterogeneous** societies than in **homogeneous** ones, **simply** because there are more **diverse points of view available** in the **former.** There are more ideas, more **conflicts** of interest, and more groups and organizations of different **persuasions.** In addition, there is usually a greater worldly interest and **tolerance** in heterogeneous societies. All these factors tend to promote social change by opening more areas of life to decision rather than **subjecting** them to authority. In a quite homogeneous society, there are fewer occasions for people to **perceive** the need or the opportunity for change, because everything seems to be the same and, if not satisfactory, at least customary and **undisputed.**

Within a society, social change is also likely to occur more frequently and more **readily** (1) in the material aspects of the culture than in the nonmaterial, for example, in technology rather than in **values;** (2) in what has been learned later in life rather than what was learned early; (3) in the less basic, less emotional, or less **sacred** aspects of society than in their opposites, like religion or a system of **prestige;** (4) in the simple elements rather than in the complex ones; (5) in form rather than in **substance;** and (6) in elements **congenial** to the culture rather than in strange elements.

Furthermore, social change is easier if it is gradual. For example, it comes more readily in human relations on a **continuous** scale rather than one with **sharp** dichotomies. This is one reason why change has not come more quickly to Black Americans as compared to other American **minorities,** because of the sharp difference in appearance between them and their white **counterparts.**

COMPREHENSION EXERCISES

Exercise 1

1. What are the elements of the main contrast in the first paragraph in Passage B?

   a. ______________________________

   b. ______________________________

In the first paragraph of Passage B the author contrasts two kinds of societies by giving the contrasting characteristics of each. Below is a list of these characteristics. In each blank write "HET" if it is a characteristic of heterogeneous societies and "HOM" if it is a characteristic of homogeneous societies.

_______ 2. More different points of view are available.

_______ 3. There are fewer occasions to perceive the need for change.

_______ 4. There are more ideas.

_______ 5. There is usually a greater worldly interest.

_______ 6. Everything seems to be the same.

_______ 7. People accept things without dispute.

_______ 8. People can make more decisions.

_______ 9. Many things are subject to authority.

_______ 10. There are many groups and organizations of different persuasions.

_______ 11. People are usually more tolerant.

_______ 12. There are more conflicts of interest.

Exercise 2

In the second paragraph of Passage B, the author mentions those aspects of culture that are likely to change readily and those that are not. In the blanks below, write "likely" for those aspects that are likely to change readily and "not likely" for those aspects that are not likely to change readily.

1. ____________________ material
2. ____________________ technology
3. ____________________ nonmaterial
4. ____________________ values
5. ____________________ things learned early
6. ____________________ less basic
7. ____________________ less emotional
8. ____________________ less sacred
9. ____________________ religion

10. ______________________ system of prestige
11. ______________________ things learned later in life
12. ______________________ simple elements
13. ______________________ substance
14. ______________________ complex elements
15. ______________________ form

VOCABULARY EXERCISES

Exercise 3

Find the word in the list that best completes each sentence and write it in the blank.

available	heterogeneous	prestige
conflicts	homogeneous	subject
counterparts	minority	tolerance
diverse	perceive	undisputed

1. There are people of different occupations, social backgrounds and interests in this group; it is a ______________________ group.
2. Saudi Arabia produces more petroleum annually than any other country in the world and is the ______________________ leader in petroleum production.
3. An example of a ______________________ society is a small village, where the people have similar occupations, interests, and beliefs.
4. Most of your necessities are ______________________ in a modern supermarket.
5. In a heterogeneous society, people often disagree with each other, and this often leads to ______________________.
6. World leaders must have a great deal of understanding and ______________________ for opinions that differ from their own.
7. The American negotiators at the conference were forced to wait for their Russian ______________________ to return.
8. The office of prime minister has a great deal of ______________________.

9. Most governments ______________________ high officials to a careful security examination.
10. While Spanish is the national language in many countries, native Spanish-speaking people are a ______________________ in the United States.
11. Many people do not ______________________ the need for change.
12. A heterogeneous society consists of people with ______________________ interests, backgrounds, and occupations.

Exercise 4

Fill in each blank below with the correct word from the list. Each word is used only once.

available	heterogeneous	prestige
conflicts	homogeneous	subject
counterparts	minority	tolerance
diverse	perceive	undisputed

In ______________________ societies people have similar ideas and beliefs, whereas in ______________________ ones, ______________________ points of view are ______________________. While there are more ideas and more ______________________ in interest, there is also usually more ______________________ for different opinions. In the former type of society, people are not likely to ______________________ the need or the opportunity for change. Most values are ______________________, and decisions are ______________________ to authority. Social change occurs more frequently in the material aspects of culture than in the nonmaterial, such as values or systems of ______________________. In heterogeneous societies, members of ______________________ groups may find that change occurs less rapidly than for their ______________________ in the majority group.

WORD SKILLS

The prefix *non-*

Example from Passage B: *non*material (ll. 12–13)

The prefix *non-* is added to nouns or adjectives and means "not."

Examples: *Word*	*Meaning*
noncooperation	failure to cooperate
nonproductive	not productive

Exercise 5

Fill in each blank below with the word from the list that best completes the sentence.

nonessential	nonprofit	nonstop
nonexistent	nonsense	

1. This organization does not make a profit. It is a ______________________ organization.
2. It is often difficult to understand the speech of very young children, and their words sometimes sound like ______________________.
3. There are no living things on the moon. Life is ______________________ there.
4. Some companies produce goods that are not really necessary. Many such ______________________ products, however, greatly improve the quality of life.
5. This flight is ______________________. It makes no stops on its way to New York.

DISCOURSE SKILLS

Exercise 6

In Passage B, there are many comparative constructions. In some of these, the elements and criterion are mentioned, or *explicitly* stated.

Example: Social change is (more likely) to occur in heterogeneous societies (than) in homogeneous ones. (ll. 1–2)

Criterion: Social change ... to occur
Element 1: in heterogeneous societies
Element 2: in homogeneous ones

In some cases, the **elements** of the comparison or contrast are not mentioned.

Example: There are more ideas, more conflicts in interest, and more groups and organizations of different persuasions. (ll. 3–4)

In this sentence, the **elements** of the comparison are not explicitly stated. The elements "in heterogeneous societies" and "in homogeneous societies" are implied, or *implicit.*

There are (more) ideas, (more) conflicts of interest . . .

Criteria

[in heterogeneous societies] than [in homogeneous ones.]

[Implicit Element 1] [Implicit Element 2]

In other cases, the **criterion** of the comparison or contrast is implicit.

Example: [social change is (more likely) to occur] in the simple elements

[Implicit Criterion] Element 1

rather than in the complex ones. (ll. 16–17)

Element 2

In each exercise below, circle the comparative marker or write it in the blank. Then write the elements and the criterion of the comparison or contrast in the blanks. Place those that are implicit in brackets [ ]. Find the answers by referring to Passage B.

1. There are more different points of view available in the former.

   Element 1: ______________________________

   Element 2: ______________________________

   Criterion: ______________________________

2. There are more groups and organizations of different persuasions.

   Element 1: ______________________________

   Element 2. ______________________________

   Criterion: ______________________________

3. There is usually a greater worldly interest and tolerance in heterogeneous societies.

   Element 1: ______________________________

Element 2: ______________________

Criterion: ______________________

4. More areas of life are open to decision rather than subject to authority.

   Element 1: ______________________

   Element 2: ______________________

   Criterion: ______________________

5. In a quite homogeneous society, there are fewer occasions for people to perceive the need or the opportunity for change.

   Element 1: ______________________

   Element 2: ______________________

   Criterion: ______________________

   ____

6. Social change is likely to occur more readily in the material aspects of culture rather than in the nonmaterial.

   Element 1: ______________________

   Element 2: ______________________

   Criterion: ______________________

7. in what was learned later in life rather than what was learned early

   Element 1: ______________________

   Element 2: ______________________

   Criterion: ______________________

   Marker: ______________________

8. in the less basic, less emotional, or less sacred rather than in their opposites

   Element 1: ______________________

   Element 2: ______________________

   Criterion: ______________________

   Marker: ______________________

9. in the simple elements rather than the complex ones

   Element 1: ______________________

   Element 2: ______________________

Criterion: ______________________________

Marker: ______________________________

10. in form rather than in substance

Element 1: ______________________________

Element 2: ______________________________

Criterion: ______________________________

Marker: ______________________________

11. It comes more readily in human relations on a continuous scale rather than one with sharp dichotomies.

Element 1: ______________________________

Element 2: ______________________________

Criterion: ______________________________

Exercise 7

In most comparative or contrastive constructions, an unequal relationship between the two elements can be expressed in at least two different ways.

Example: Social change is **more** likely to occur in heterogeneous societies (Element 1) than in homogeneous ones (Element 2).

This means the same as:

Social change is **less** likely to occur in homogeneous societies (Element 2) than in heterogeneous ones (Element 1).

In the second sentence of the example, a comparative marker with the opposite meaning is used, and the order of the two elements is reversed.

In each of the sentences below, underline the elements of the comparison or contrast, circle the comparative marker, and underline the criterion twice. Then rewrite the sentence, expressing the meaning in a different way, according to the example above.

1. There are more different points of view in heterogeneous societies than in homogeneous ones.

   There are ______________ in ______________ than in ______________.

2. In a heterogeneous society there is usually a greater worldly interest than in a homogeneous one.

   In ______________ there is usually a ______________ worldly interest than in ______________.

3. In a quite homogeneous society, there are fewer occasions for people to perceive the need for change than in a heterogeneous society.

   In a ______________ there are ______________ occasions for people to perceive the need for change than in a ______________.

4. Social change is likely to occur more frequently in the material aspects of culture than in the nonmaterial ones.

   Social change is likely to occur ______________ in the ______________ aspects of culture than in the ______________ ones.

5. Social change is easier if it is gradual, rather than sudden.

   Social change is ______________ if it is ______________ rather than ______________.

6. Social change comes more readily on a continuous scale rather than on one with sharp dichotomies.

   Social change comes ______________ on a ______________ scale rather than on a ______________ scale.

7. Social change has occurred less quickly with Black Americans as compared with other American minorities.

   Social change has occurred ______________ with ______________ as compared with ______________.

READING EXERCISE

Read the following passage and then do the exercises that follow.

Within the United States there are a number of differences in behavior associated with urban and rural residence. There are more foreign immigrants in cities than in rural areas. While there is more political and religious tolerance in the cities, there is more religious observance in rural areas. There is generally a higher level of education in the cities, along with greater social change, whereas rural society tends to be more stable. Rural areas have a greater proportion of married people as well as a lower divorce rate. Finally, while there is more crime in the cities, there are probably more crimes of violence, proportionately, in rural areas.

Adapted from Bernard Berelson and Gary A. Steiner, 1967

Exercise 8

In each blank below, write the word from the Reading Exercise passage that has nearly the same meaning as the **boldface** word or phrase.

1. The population of the United States includes great numbers of **people who have come from other countries to settle.**

   ____

2. Rural societies tend to be more **fixed** than urban ones.

   ____

3. A larger proportion of people in cities than in the country **end their marriages.**

   ____

4. There are many differences between cities and rural areas in people's **way of acting.**

   ____

5. The **use of great force to cause harm** is proportionately more common in the country than in cities.

   ____

6. In cities, people change **the place where they live** relatively often.

   ____

Exercise 9

Answer the following questions, based on the Reading Exercise passage.

1. What is the main generalization of the passage?

____

____

2. What two elements are contrasted in the passage?

____

____

3. Where would one be more free to practice his or her own religion?

____

4. Where would you expect to find traditional values maintained?

____

5. Where is one more likely to be badly hurt by a criminal?

____

Lesson 14

West Germany's Trade Surplus with OPEC

PREREADING ACTIVITIES

A. Discussion Questions

1. What goods or services does your country produce that it can sell and send to other countries?
2. What goods or services must it buy and bring in from other countries?
3. What happens when a country buys and brings in more goods from other countries than it sells and sends out to other countries?
4. Does this create a problem for the country's economy? Why?
5. What actions could a country take to change this situation?

B. Special Vocabulary (Marked "*" in Passage A)

billion	the number 1,000,000,000 (in British usage, 1,000,000,000,000)
mark	the unit of currency in West Germany

C. Guide Questions
As you read Passage A, ask yourself the following questions.

1. Why was 1977 an important year for the West German economy?
2. What two things did that country do to record a trade surplus?

3. What was the most important factor in West Germany's success in recording a trade surplus?
4. The cost of oil brought into West Germany is given for what three years?
5. What happened to the amount of goods sent by West Germany to OPEC countries from 1975 through 1977?
6. Which increased more from 1975 through 1977, goods sent from West Germany to OPEC or to the entire world?
7. What may West German companies try to do in the future?

NOW READ PASSAGE A. WHEN YOU FINISH READING, ANSWER THE GUIDE QUESTIONS.

READING PASSAGES

West Germany's Trade Surplus with OPEC

Adapted from *Kayhan International,* Feb. 12, 1978

Passage A

West Germany **reduced** the costs of **bringing in** oil **from other countries** by **increasing** the amount of capital goods it **sent to other countries** and recorded its first-ever trade surplus with the Organization of Petroleum Exporting Countries (OPEC) in 1977. West Germany **announced** a 1.6 *billion *mark trade surplus with OPEC in 1977, as compared with a 3.7 billion mark trade **shortage** in 1976 and a 13.3 billion mark trade shortage in 1974. The trade surplus **brings attention to** the West German success in **stopping** rises in the **need** for energy and in **moving** the regional **foundation** of its markets **outside** Germany to the OPEC countries, following the 1973 oil price increase.

The **most important** factor in the West German success has been the lack of any increase in the oil brought into Germany. In 1977, West Germany brought in about 97 billion tons of oil, **a reduction** from the 99.2 billion tons brought in during 1976. The cost of the oil brought in from OPEC has also remained basically **unchanged.** In 1977, the oil brought in from OPEC **added up** to 23.3 billion marks, **a small** reduction from the 24.4 billion marks spent in 1976 and the 23.8 billion marks spent in 1974.

While the amount of oil West Germany brings in from OPEC has remained unchanged, the goods which West Germany sends to OPEC countries have continued to increase. Products sent to OPEC countries accounted for only 4.5 percent of those West Germany sent to the entire world in 1974, but this increased to 7.5 percent in 1975 and 8.0 percent in 1976. In 1977, West German products sent to OPEC countries accounted for 9.1 percent, or about

24.9 billion marks of the country's 273.5 billion marks worth of products sent to the entire world.

The growth of West German products sent to OPEC countries is even more impressive when compared with the **yearly** growth in the products West Germany sends to the entire world. In 1975, West German products sent to OPEC countries grew by 59.0 percent, while West German products sent to the entire world were 3.8 percent **less than** the year **before.** In 1976, products sent to OPEC increased 24.0 percent, **compared to** a growth of 16.0 percent for West German products sent to the world as a whole. In 1977, products sent to OPEC grew 20.0 percent, while products sent to the world as a whole grew only 6.5 percent. These **statistics** may indicate that West German companies are going to continue to try to **increase** the amount of goods they send to OPEC countries. If these trends continue, it is **not likely** that West Germany will have trade deficits with OPEC countries in the future.

Passage B

West Germany, by **cutting** the cost of oil **imports** with **rising** capital goods **exports,** recorded its first-ever trade surplus with the Organization of Petroleum Exporting Countries (OPEC) in 1977. West Germany **posted** a 1.6 billion mark trade surplus with OPEC in 1977, compared with a 3.7 billion mark trade **deficit** in 1976 and a 13.3 billion mark trade deficit in 1974. The trade surplus **emphasizes** the West German success at **curbing** rises in energy **demand** and **shifting** the regional **basis** of its export markets following the 1973 oil price increase.

The **prime** factor in the West German success has been the lack of any increase in oil imports. In 1977, West Germany imported about 97 billion tons of oil, **down** from 99.2 billion tons in 1976. The cost of the oil imports from OPEC has also remained basically **constant.** In 1977, oil imports from OPEC **totaled** 23.3 billion marks, down **slightly** from 24.4 billion marks in 1976 and 23.8 billion marks in 1974.

While West German oil imports from OPEC have remained constant, German exports to OPEC countries have continued to increase. Exports to OPEC countries accounted for only 4.5 percent of West Germany's total world exports in 1974, but rose to 7.5 percent in 1975 and 8.0 percent in 1976. In 1977, West German exports to OPEC countries accounted for 9.1 percent, or about 24.9 billion marks of the country's 273.5 billion marks in total world exports.

The growth of West German exports to OPEC countries is even more impressive when compared with the **year-to-year** growth in total West German exports. In 1975 West German exports to OPEC countries grew by 59.0 percent, while West German exports as a whole were **off** 3.8 percent from the **previous** year. In 1976, exports to OPEC climbed 24.0 percent **against** a growth of 16.0 percent for West German exports as a whole. In 1977, exports to

OPEC grew 20.0 percent, while exports as a whole grew only 6.5 percent. These **figures** may indicate that West German companies are going to continue to try to **boost** their exports to OPEC countries. If these trends continue, it is **improbable** that West Germany will record trade deficits with OPEC countries in the future.

COMPREHENSION EXERCISES

Exercise 1

Reread Passage B and then answer the following questions.

1. One sentence in the first paragraph tells you what the entire passage is about. What is the main topic of the passage?

2. What is the main generalization of the second paragraph?

3. What information is given to support this generalization?

   a.

   b.

4. What is the main generalization of the third paragraph?

5. What information is given to support this generalization?

6. What is the main generalization of the fourth paragraph?

7. What information is given to support this generalization?

8. What tentative conclusion does the author come to in the fourth paragraph?

____

____

Exercise 2

Sometimes an author will use **synonyms**—different words that have nearly the same meaning—to avoid repetition. In Passage B, the author discusses both *increases* and *decreases* and uses several different words that have nearly the same meaning as these terms. In the blanks below, write "INC" if the word means *increase* and "DEC" if the word means *decrease*.

_______ 1. cutting (l. 1)

_______ 2. rising (l. 1)

_______ 3. curbing (l. 6)

_______ 4. down from (l. 11)

_______ 5. rose (l. 18)

_______ 6. growth (l. 22)

_______ 7. grew (l. 24)

_______ 8. off (l. 25)

_______ 9. climbed (l. 26)

_______ 10. boost (l. 30)

VOCABULARY EXERCISES

Exercise 3

Find the word from the list that best matches each definition below and write it in the blank.

basis	exports	prime
constant	imports	shift
deficit	previous	

1. ____________________ goods brought in from abroad
2. ____________________ unchanged or unchanging

3. ______________ to move from one place or position to another
4. ______________ the amount by which something is less than expected; shortage
5. ______________ foundation; principle
6. ______________ goods sent to other countries
7. ______________ first in importance or degree
8. ______________ occurring before something else

Exercise 4

Fill in each blank below with the correct word from the list. Some words are used more than once.

basis	exports	prime
constant	imports	shifting
deficits	previous	

West Germany's 1977 trade surplus with OPEC countries emphasizes its success in curbing increases in oil ______________ and in ______________ the regional ______________ of its ______________. In ______________ years, West Germany's oil ______________ from OPEC were greater than its ______________ to OPEC countries, resulting in trade ______________. From 1974 through 1977, however, West Germany was able to hold the cost of oil imports nearly ______________. Thus, although the cost of oil imports totaled 23.8 billion marks in 1974, the cost of oil imports was only 23.3 billion marks in 1977. This lack of any increase in oil imports has been the ______________ factor in West Germany's success.

WORD SKILLS

The prefixes *in-*, *im-*, *ir-*, and *il-*

Example from Passage B: *im*probable (l. 31)

The prefixes *in-*, *im-*, *ir-*, and *il-* are added to adjectives and nouns. They add the meaning "not" or "the opposite of."

Spelling Note: *im-* occurs only before "b," "m," and "p."
***ir-* occurs only before "r."**
***il-* occurs only before "l."**

Examples:	*Base*	*Word*	*Meaning*
	ability	inability	lack of ability
	direct	indirect	not direct
	literate	illiterate	not literate
	possible	impossible	not possible
	regular	irregular	not regular

Exercise 5

Add the appropriate prefix (*in-*, *im-*, *ir-*, or *il-*) to each of the following words and then write them in the correct blanks below.

adequate practical
complete replaceable
legal

1. It is ______________________ to steal an automobile.
2. There is a shortage of housing because the supply of building materials is ______________________.
3. We have not finished the report yet, and do not want to submit an ______________________ annual report of the company's condition.
4. There is no other piece of equipment like this. It is ______________________.
5. The production costs of this new machine are greater than its possible sale price, so it is ______________________ to produce.

DISCOURSE SKILLS

Exercise 6

Reread Passage B and then answer the following questions.

1. Why was 1977 a successful year for the West German economy?

____

2. Did West Germany have a trade deficit or a trade surplus in 1976?

____

3. Was there a deficit or a surplus in 1974?

____

4. Using the information given in the first paragraph of Passage B, complete the following table:

Year	Trade	Amount
a. ________	____________________	____________________
b. ________	____________________	____________________
c. ________	____________________	____________________

5. Was the difference in amount between 1974 and 1976 larger or smaller than that between 1976 and 1977?

____

6. In the first paragraph in Passage B, the author is making contrast. What are the three **elements** of the contrast?

____________________, ____________________,

____

7. What is the **criterion** of the contrast?

____

8. What is the **marker** of the contrast?

____

9. Using the information provided in the **second** paragraph of Passage B, complete the following table:

Year	Cost of Oil Imports from OPEC
a. ________	____________________
b. ________	____________________
c. ________	____________________

10. In the second paragraph, the author is making a contrast. What are the three **elements** of the contrast?

____________________, ____________________,

____

11. What is the **criterion** of the contrast?

____

Exercise 7

1. According to the third paragraph, what is the major contrast between West German oil **imports** from OPEC and West German **exports** to OPEC?

____

____

2. What word is the **marker** of this contrast?

____

3. In 1974, what percentage of West Germany's total world exports went to OPEC?

____

4. In 1974, what percentage went to the rest of the world?

____

5. In the third paragraph, the author uses percentages to contrast two elements. What are the two elements of this contrast?

____

____

6. In 1975, what percentage of West Germany's total world exports went to OPEC?

____

7. Using the information provided in the third paragraph, complete the following table:

Year	Percentage Exports to OPEC
a. ________	________________
b. ________	________________
c. ________	________________
d. ________	________________

8. Was the increase in percentage of exports to OPEC larger in 1976 or in 1977?

    ____

9. In the third paragraph, the author contrasts four elements with respect to the same criterion. What are the four **elements**?

    ____________________, ____________________,

    ____________________, ____________________

10. What is the **criterion** of the contrast?

    ____

Exercise 8

In the first sentence of the fourth paragraph, the author uses a contrastive construction to state a *general* contrast. In the blanks below, identify the **elements** of this contrast, the **criterion,** and the **contrastive marker.**

1. Element 1: ______________________________

    ____

2. Element 2: ______________________________

    ____

3. Criterion: ______________________________

4. Marker: ______________________________

    To illustrate this general contrast, the author gives several *specific* contrasts.

5. How much did West German exports to OPEC increase in 1975?

    ________ percent

6. How much did West German total world exports decrease in 1975?

    ________ percent

7. In 1975, what was the difference between the increase in exports to OPEC and the decrease in total world exports?

    ________ percent

8. Using the information provided in the fourth paragraph, complete the following chart:

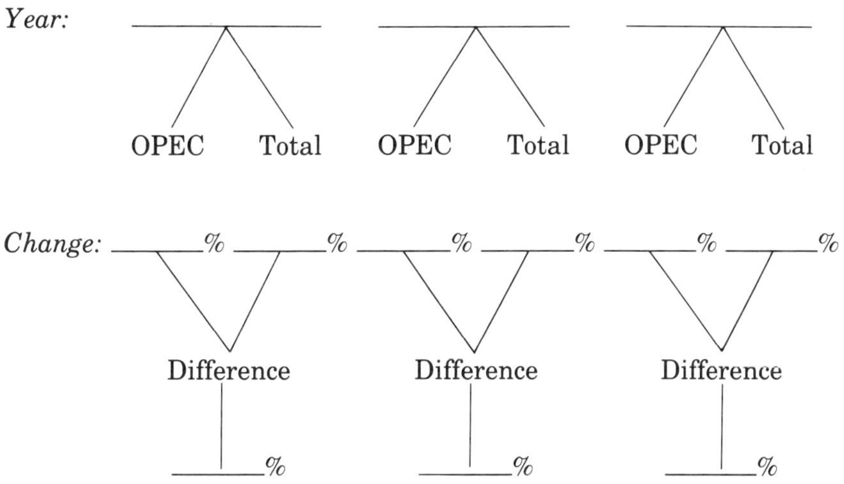

9. What are the elements of the *specific* contrast for 1975?

____

____

10. What is the criterion of the contrast?

____

11. What are the elements of the *specific* contrast for 1977?

____

____

12. What is the criterion of the contrast?

____

13. What are the three elements that illustrate the *general* contrast made in the fourth paragraph?

____________________, ____________________,

____

14. What is the criterion of these contrasts?

____

____

READING EXERCISE

Read the following passage and then do the exercises that follow.

Three of the world's smallest countries—Kuwait, the United Arab Emirates (UAE), and Qatar—have the highest average incomes per person, according to a 1976 World Bank publication which measures income, output, and world populations. The small populations of these countries, combined with their tremendous oil wealth, resulted in a per capita income during 1976 of $15,480 in Kuwait, $13,990 in the UAE, and $11,400 in Qatar. By contrast, Bhutan, the tiny kingdom surrounded by India and Tibet, was the world's poorest country with a per capita income of only $70.

The publication also shows that the richest of the industrial countries, Sweden, had an income of $8,670 per person, followed by the United States at $7,890, and West Germany with $7,380. Europe, including the Soviet Union, remained the world's richest continent, with only two countries—Albania and Turkey—having per capita incomes of less than $1,000.

In contrast, most people in Africa and Asia continue to live in poverty, with only a handful of countries in both continents having an income of more than $1,000 per person. Japan was the richest non-oil producing nation in Asia, with an annual income of $4,910 per head. This contrasts sharply with Bangladesh's $110, India's $150, and China's $410.

Adapted from *Kayhan International,* Feb. 18, 1978

Exercise 9

In each blank below, write the word from the Reading Exercise passage that has nearly the same meaning as the **boldface** word or phrase in the sentence.

1. The annual per capita incomes of Qatar and Bhutan are **clearly** different.

   ____

2. A **small number** of the world's smallest countries have the highest per capita incomes.

   ____

3. Some countries have **very great** incomes from oil.

   ____

4. **The condition of being poor** could be greatly reduced through greater cooperation among the nations of the world.

 ____

5. A country's income **per person** depends on its total national income and its population.

 ____

Exercise 10

Answer the following questions, based on the Reading Exercise passage.

1. What two factors combined to make Kuwait, the UAE, and Qatar the richest countries in the world?

 ____

 ____

2. How are these two factors used to determine the average per capita income of a country?

 ____

 ____

3. How did the per capita income of India compare with that of Bhutan?

 ____

4. How did the per capita income of Sweden contrast with that of Japan?

 ____

5. What country had the second highest per capita income among the industrial countries?

 ____

6. What two continents were still the world's poorest?

 ____

 ____

Lesson 15

Is War Inevitable?

PREREADING ACTIVITIES

A. Discussion Questions

1. In what ways can individuals or groups work together to help each other when there is not enough land, food, jobs, or other necessities for all?
2. In this kind of situation, do individuals or groups sometimes act against each other's interests?
3. What different forms may these actions take?
4. How would you define the word "competition"?
5. How would you define the word "conflict"? How is it different from "competition"?
6. Do you think it is impossible for some groups or some individuals to avoid conflict? Why, or why not?
7. What actions can individuals or groups take to try to avoid war?

B. Guide Questions
As you read Passage A, ask yourself the following questions.

1. What two types of opposition are defined in the first paragraph?
2. Why does the author feel it is necessary to define these words?
3. According to the author, can conflict be avoided?

4. Why do many authors believe that war cannot be avoided?
5. Is animals' struggle for existence a form of conflict or of competition?
6. What is the author's main point in this passage?

NOW READ PASSAGE A. WHEN YOU FINISH READING, ANSWER THE GUIDE QUESTIONS.

READING PASSAGES

Is War Inevitable?

Adapted from Joel Larus, 1966

Passage A

The question of whether war **cannot be avoided** is one which has concerned many of the world's great writers. Before considering this question, it will be useful to introduce some related **ideas.** The **meaning** of *conflict* can be **stated** as opposition among social **units**—groups or individuals—directed against one another. This is distinguished from *competition,* which **means** opposition among social units independently **seeking to obtain** something which is in inadequate supply. Competitors may not **know about** one another, while **those who participate** in a conflict do. Conflict and competition are both **classes** of *opposition.* The **meaning** of *opposition* has been **stated** as a process by which social units **perform activities** in the disservice of one another. Opposition is thus contrasted to *cooperation,* the **process** by which social units **act** in the service of one another. These **specifications of meaning** are necessary because it is important to emphasize that competition between individuals or groups **cannot be avoided** in a world of limited resources, but conflict can. Conflict, nevertheless, is very likely to occur and is probably an essential and desirable element of human societies.

Many authors have based their arguments that war cannot be avoided on the **idea** that in the struggle for existence among **groups** of animals, only those which are **best adapted remain alive.** In general, however, this struggle in nature is competition, not conflict. Social animals, such as monkeys and cattle, fight to win or maintain leadership of the group. The struggle for existence does not occur in fights such as these, but in the competition for limited feeding areas and for the occupancy of areas free from meat-eating animals. Those who fail in this competition either starve to death or **are killed** by other types of animals. This struggle for existence is not **similar to** human war, but is like the competition of individuals for jobs, markets, and materials. The **most important quality** of this struggle is the competition for the necessities of life that are **not enough** to satisfy all.

Among nations, there is competition in developing resources, trades, skills, and a satisfactory way of life. The successful nations grow and **become wealthy;** the unsuccessful decline. While it is true that this competition may **cause** efforts to expand territory at the expense of others, and thus lead to conflict, it is also true that warlike conflict among nations can be avoided. Competition, however, cannot be avoided.

NOW GO BACK AND ANSWER THE GUIDE QUESTIONS.

Passage B

The question of whether war is **inevitable** is one which has concerned many of the world's great writers. Before considering this question, it will be useful to introduce some related **concepts.** *Conflict,* **defined** as opposition among social **entities** directed against one another, is distinguished from *competition,* **defined** as opposition among social entities independently **striving for** something which is in inadequate supply. Competitors may not be **aware** of one another, while the **parties** to a conflict are. Conflict and competition are both **categories** of *opposition,* which has been **defined** as a process by which social entities **function** in the disservice of one another. Opposition is thus contrasted with *cooperation,* the process by which social entities **function** in the service of one another. These **definitions** are necessary because it is important to emphasize that competition between individuals or groups is **inevitable** in a world of limited resources, but conflict is not. Conflict, nevertheless, is very likely to occur, and is probably an essential and desirable element of human societies.

Many authors have argued for the inevitability of war from the **premise** that in the struggle for existence among animal **species,** only the **fittest survive.** In general, however, this struggle in nature is competition, not conflict. Social animals, such as monkeys and cattle, fight to win or maintain leadership of the group. The struggle for existence occurs not in such fights, but in the competition for limited feeding areas and for the occupancy of areas free from meat-eating animals. Those who fail in this competition starve to death or become **victims** to other species. This struggle for existence does not **resemble** human war, but rather the competition of individuals for jobs, markets, and materials. The **essence** of the struggle is the competition for the necessities of life that are **insufficient** to satisfy all.

Among nations there is competition in developing resources, trades, skills, and a satisfactory way of life. The successful nations grow and **prosper;** the unsuccessful decline. While it is true that this competition may **induce** efforts to expand territory at the expense of others, and thus lead to conflict, it cannot be said that war-like conflict among nations is inevitable, although competition is.

COMPREHENSION EXERCISE

Exercise 1

Reread Passage B and then answer the following questions.

Paragraph 1

1. How does the author define "opposition"?

____

____

2. What are two differences between "conflict" and "competition"?

____

____

3. How are "conflict" and "competition" similar?

____

4. How is "opposition" different from "cooperation"?

____

5. How are "opposition" and "cooperation" similar?

____

Paragraph 2

6. What example of conflict among animals does the author give?

____

7. What example of competition among animals does the author give?

____

8. What examples of human competition does the author give?

____

____

____

9. Why is competition for necessities such as these inevitable?

____

____

Paragraph 3

10. What examples of competition among nations does the author give?

____

____

____

11. What may this competition induce?

____

VOCABULARY EXERCISES

Exercise 2

In each blank below, write the word from the list that best matches the definition.

aware	essence	premise
category	function	resemble
concept	induce	survive
define	inevitable	victim
entity	parties	

1. _______________ to remain alive or unhurt
2. _______________ to be similar to
3. _______________ not possible to avoid or prevent
4. _______________ persons who participate in an activity
5. _______________ a statement or idea that is the basis for an argument or a conclusion
6. _______________ having knowledge or realization of something
7. _______________ an animal or person that is killed or hurt
8. _______________ a division or class
9. _______________ to cause
10. _______________ something that exists independently
11. _______________ to perform a specified action
12. _______________ a general idea
13. _______________ the most important quality of something
14. _______________ to state or specify the meaning of something

Exercise 3

Fill in each blank below with a word from the list. Each word is used only once.

aware	essence	premise
categories	function	resembles
concepts	induce	survive
define	inevitable	victims
entities	parties	

Many writers believe that war is ______________ and have based their argument on the ______________ that human war ______________ the struggle for existence among animals. In this struggle, the species which are the fittest ______________, while those which are weak become the ______________ of other animal species. It is necessary to ______________ two ______________ in order to better understand the nature of this struggle: *conflict* and *competition.* In conflict, the ______________ involved ______________ in opposition against each other and are ______________ of each other. In competition, on the other hand, the individual ______________ act independently to obtain something and may not know about each other. Conflict and competition are thus two ______________ of opposition. The ______________ of animals' struggle for survival is the competition for necessities which are inadequate for all. In some cases, competition may be strong enough to ______________ conflict, although this can generally be avoided. Thus, although competition is inevitable, war is not.

WORD SKILLS

A. The suffixes *-ant* and *-ent*

Example from Passage B: insuffici*ent* (l. 26)

The suffixes *-ant* and *-ent* are added to verbs to form nouns or adjectives.

Examples:	*Verb*	*Noun*	*Adjective*
	appear	xxxxxxxxx	apparent*
	assist	assistant	xxxxxxxxx
	defend	defendant	xxxxxxxxx

*Note spelling change.

Exercise 4

Fill in the blanks below with the correct verb forms of the underlined words.

1. Many people are ignorant about the world outside their own country.

   Many people ______________________ the world outside their own country.
2. Prof. Johnson always writes excellent reports.

   Prof. Johnson ______________________ in writing reports.
3. All people should be obedient to the laws of the country.

   All people should ______________________ the laws of the country.
4. Achievement in college is dependent upon many variables.

   Achievement in college ______________________ upon many variables.
5. Ms. Morely is president of our Middle East office.

   Ms. Morley ______________________ over our Middle East office.

B. The noun suffixes -*ance* and -*ence*

Example from Passage B: exist*ence* (l. 17)

The suffixes -*ance* and -*ence* are added to verbs to form nouns.

Examples:	*Verb*	*Noun*
	appear	appearance
	ignore	ignorance*

*Note spelling change.

Exercise 5

Fill in the blanks below with the correct noun form, ending in -*ance* or -*ence,* of the verb in parentheses.

1. (differ) Tomas' parents noticed a ____________________ in their son's behavior when he returned from college.
2. (disappear) The young girl's ____________________ was a mystery to everyone.
3. (perform) The actress gave an excellent ____________________ last night.
4. (refer) Kazumi made a ____________________ to you in his letter.
5. (attend) The lecture was almost empty, and the professor was disappointed by the poor ____________________.

C. The noun suffixes *-ancy* and *-ency*

Example from Passage B: occup*ancy* (l. 21)

The suffixes -*ancy* and -*ency* are added to adjectives or verbs to form nouns.

Examples:	*Verb or Adjective*	*Nouns*
	efficient (adj.)	efficiency*
	expect (v.)	expectancy

*Note spelling change.

Exercise 6

Fill in the blanks below with the correct noun form of the verb in parentheses.

1. (frequent) What is the ____________________ of traffic accidents in your city?
2. (consistent) There is no ____________________ in the foreign policy of some countries.
3. (emerge) The government declared a state of ____________________ during the floods last year.
4. (expect) The life ____________________ for a person in the United States is over 60 years.
5. (occupy) What is the percentage of ____________________ for these apartments?

DISCOURSE SKILLS

Exercise 7

A **definition** consists of three components:

The **term** that is being defined
The general **class** to which the term belongs
The **distinguishing characteristic** of the term

Examples: *Supply* (term) is the *amount of goods or services* (class) that is *available for purchase.* (distinguishing characteristic)

Demand (term) is the *amount of goods or services* (class) that *people are willing and able to purchase.* (distinguishing characteristic)

Reread Passage B, and then answer the following.

1. To what class does the term *conflict* belong?

____

2. What is its distinguishing characteristic?

____

3. Write a definition of *conflict.*

   Conflict is ______________________

   that is ______________________

4. To what class does the term *competition* belong?

____

5. What is its distinguishing characteristic?

____

6. Write a definition of *competition.*

   Competition is ______________________

   in which ______________________.

7. To what class does the term *opposition* belong?

   ____

8. What is its distinguishing characteristic?

   ____

9. Write a definition of *opposition*.

   Opposition is ______________________________

   in which ____________________________________.

10. To what class does the term *cooperation* belong?

    ____

11. What is its distinguishing characteristic?

    ____

12. Write a definition of *cooperation*.

    Cooperation is ______________________________

    in which ____________________________________.

Exercise 8

Complete the following chart, using your answers to Exercise 7.

____
Class

Term: ____________________ ____________________

Distinguishing characteristics: ____________________ ____________________

____________________ ____________________

Term: ____________________ ____________________

Distinguishing characteristics: ____________________ ____________________

____________________ ____________________

Exercise 9

In the following sentences, circle the term being defined, underline the class to which it belongs, and draw two lines under its distinguishing characteristic.

1. A partnership is a business contract in which two or more parties agree to furnish part of the capital and to share in the profits and losses.
2. A political party is a group of individuals organized to promote specific principles and to elect certain candidates to public office.
3. A bicycle is a two-wheeled vehicle.
4. Any process by which social entities function in the service of one another is called cooperation.
5. We can define as conflict opposition among social entities that is directed against each other.
6. Capital punishment, the penalty of death for crimes committed, is opposed by many people.
7. If the exchange of goods is conducted without the involvement of money, it is called barter.
8. Any person who was born in this country or who has become naturalized is a citizen.
9. Insects are six-legged animals.
10. For an agreement between two persons to be considered a contract, each party must agree to do something for the benefit of the other, and both parties must intend that the agreement shall be enforceable by law.

READING EXERCISE

Read the following passage and then do the exercises that follow.

The term "revolution" is often used to describe both the method of inducing change in government and the scope of the changes. In this wider sense, it means to support decisive changes in the character of government even though they do not involve violently ending an established order. In the narrower sense, the term refers exclusively to the methods used to bring about particular changes in the system of government. Here, the emphasis is on the use of violence, or extraconstitutional means, involving a temporary breakdown of the system which is being challenged and its replacement by another system or constitution. In this sense, then, revolution is an attempt to compel a change in the actual purposes of the state, by the use of force against the government legally in power. Such an attempt may succeed or it may fail. It may be brought about by an individual, a class, a religious sect, or a political party. It may aim at far-reaching and fundamental changes in the government, or it may look no further than the seizure of power from the actual holders of it. In all cases, however, the essential element in the definition is the use against the established government of force, in the sense of pressure not provided for as part of the normal working of existing institutions.

Adapted from Dorothy M. Pickles, 1967

Exercise 10

In each blank below, write the word from the Reading Exercise passage that has nearly the same meaning as the **boldface** word or phrase in the sentence.

1. There are certain **basic** human rights that all governments should strive to protect.

    ____

2. The production of automobiles was halted by a temporary **failure** of an essential piece of machinery **to function.**

    ____

3. The voters **called into question** their leader's authority to make decisions without considering their interests.

    ____

4. This property belongs **only** to our employees and to **no others.**

    ____

5. Only after several years was the **extent** of the damage known.

    ____

6. The committee's report gave **special importance** to the dangers of nuclear war.

    ____

7. If Mr. Williams cannot attend the meeting, we should find **someone to take his place.**

    ____

8. In some instances, it is necessary to **force** people to obey the law.

    ____

Exercise 11

Answer the following questions, based on the Reading Exercise passage.

1. To what does the word "revolution" refer in its wider sense?

____

____

2. To what does the word refer exclusively, in its narrower sense?

____

3. What is emphasized, in this sense?

____

4. Are revolutions always successful?

____

5. What groups may cause a revolution?

____

____

____

6. What may be the aim of revolution?

____

____

7. What kind of force is the essential element of the narrow definition of "revolution"?

____

Lesson 16

Bureaucracy

PREREADING ACTIVITIES

A. Discussion Questions

1. How would you describe the organization of a large government department or ministry?
2. How effectively do such organizations function?
3. What other examples of such large organizations can you think of?
4. To what extent do such large organizations influence our individual lives?
5. Do you think this influence is increasing or decreasing?
6. What are the advantages and disadvantages of this influence?

B. Special Vocabulary (Marked "*" in Passage A)

derogatory	tending to damage one's credit or character
cumbersomeness	the quality of being difficult to handle because of large size
corruption	dishonesty

C. Guide Questions

As you read Passage A, ask yourself the following questions.

1. To what does the term "bureaucracy" generally refer?
2. With what group do we usually use this term?
3. Why has the term acquired a derogatory meaning?
4. Does bureaucratization occur in public or private areas?
5. What happens to human relations as a result of bureaucratization?
6. What are some aspects of life that are influenced by bureaucracies?

NOW READ PASSAGE A. WHEN YOU FINISH READING, ANSWER THE GUIDE QUESTIONS.

READING PASSAGES

Bureaucracy

Adapted from Henry Jacoby, 1973

Passage A

Bureaucracy is an **unclear** term. Although it generally refers to a group of people concerned with organization and management, its usage is often limited to government officials. The term has also acquired a *derogatory meaning which demonstrates such **failures** in the performance of administration as slowness and *cumbersomeness.

There are many variants among bureaucracies, especially government, or state, bureaucracies. They can conduct themselves **reasonably** or **according to individual judgment.** Their performance can be efficient and precise, or lengthy and inefficient. A bureaucracy may be characterized by honesty or *corruption. Its political **direction** and social origin, as well as its status in society can vary greatly. It may function **as a group of individuals as a whole,** even if the **ranking** structure of its organization permits only a very uneven **sharing** of authority, to the **degree** that authority may not exist among the lower levels. Bureaucracy can serve as a mere tool of authority and still be significant enough to influence those in control. There have been bureaucracies, for example, which were **formed** entirely of slaves. Thus the Mamelukes were a slave bureaucracy in Egypt until they acquired full governmental power. Finally, differences exist not only between the upper and lower levels within bureaucracies, but also among subject or area specialists and administrators.

The bureaucratic *concept,* however, refers to a system of social **exchange** which **forms** in all varieties of bureaucracies and bureaucratic organizations. Franz Neumann has provided a detailed analysis: Bureaucratization, correctly understood, is a process operating in both public and private **areas,** in the state as well as in society. It means that human relations lose their directness and become **directed by people in intermediate positions.** These third parties are either public or private officials in relatively secure positions of authority. It is these people who **establish the rules** by which people must behave.[1] This has become a **widespread and inclusive** process in modern society. Neumann points out that a **huge** organizational **system** surrounds almost every aspect of human life, even including culture. Sports and the arts are also administered by professional bureaus, and special departments in the mass-media system determine how much popular music and how much classical music, how many lectures, and how much news is to be presented to the public.

Passage B

Bureaucracy is an **ambiguous** term. Although it generally refers to a group of people concerned with organization and management, its usage is often limited to government officials. The term has also acquired a derogatory meaning which points to such **shortcomings** in the performance of administration as slowness and cumbersomeness.

There are many variants among bureaucracies, especially state bureaucracies. They can conduct themselves **rationally** or **arbitrarily.** Their performance can be efficient and precise, or lengthy and inefficient. A bureaucracy may be characterized by honesty or corruption. Its political **orientation** and social origin, as well as its status in society can vary greatly. It may function **collectively,** even if its **hierarchical** structure permits only a very uneven **distribution** of authority, to the **extent** that it may be nonexistent among the lower levels. Bureaucracy can serve as the mere tool of authority and still be significant enough to influence those in control. There have been bureaucracies, for example, which have been **constituted** entirely by slaves. Thus the Mamelukes were a slave bureaucracy in Egypt until they acquired full governmental power. Finally, differences exist not only between the upper and lower levels within bureaucracies, but also between subject or area specialists and administrators.

The bureaucratic *concept,* however, refers to a system of social **interaction** which **emerges** in all varieties of bureaucracies and bureaucratic organizations. Franz Neumann has provided a detailed analysis: "Bureaucratization, correctly understood, is a process operating in both public and private **spheres,** in the state as well as in society. It means that human relations lose

[1]Franz Neumann, *Behemoth: The Structure and Practice of National Socialism* (New York and London: 1942), p. 368.

their directness and become **mediated** relations in which third parties, public or private functionaries seated more or less securely in power, authoritatively **prescribe** the behavior of man."[1] This has become a **comprehensive** process in modern society. Neumann points out that a **gigantic** organizational **network** surrounds almost every aspect of human life, even including culture. Sports and the arts are also administered by professional bureaus, and special departments in the mass-media system determine how much light and how much classical music, how many lectures, and how much news is to be presented to the public.

COMPREHENSION EXERCISE

Exercise 1

Reread Passage B and then answer the following questions.

Paragraph 1

1. What is the main point of the first paragraph?

2. How does the author define "bureaucracy"?

3. What negative characteristic of bureaucratic administration does the author mention?

4. What are two examples of this characteristic?

Paragraph 2

5. What is the main point of the second paragraph?

6. In what different ways can bureaucracies conduct themselves?

[1]Franz Neumann, *Behemoth: The Structure and Practice of National Socialism* (New York and London: 1942), p. 368.

7. In what different ways can they perform?

____

____

8. What different characteristics can they have?

____

____

9. In what ways can they differ politically and socially?

____

____

____

10. Do people at the lower levels of a bureaucratic hierarchy always have authority?

____

11. Why is this so?

____

12. Does the bureaucracy itself always have full authority?

____

13. At what levels are there differences within bureaucracies?

____

____

14. Between what types of individuals in a bureaucracy are there differences?

____

____

Paragraph 3

15. What is the main point of the third paragraph?

____

16. How does the author define the bureaucratic *concept?*

____

17. What kind of relations are characteristic of bureaucracies?

____

18. What examples are given of aspects of human life that are influenced by bureaucracies?

____

____

____

____

VOCABULARY EXERCISES

Exercise 2

In each blank below, write the word from the list that best matches the definition.

ambiguous	emerge	orientation
arbitrary	extent	prescribe
comprehensive	hierarchical	rational
constitute	network	shortcoming
distribution		

1. ____________________ direction or position relative to a given point
2. ____________________ according to reason
3. ____________________ according to the judgment or feeling of an individual; without reason
4. ____________________ a system of interconnected components
5. ____________________ to establish or determine rules for use
6. ____________________ including a wide scope or content
7. ____________________ range over which something extends; degree or amount
8. ____________________ organized or classified according to rank
9. ____________________ the dividing, sharing, or spreading out of something
10. ____________________ a lack or failure
11. ____________________ unclear; having several meanings
12. ____________________ to make up or form from parts
13. ____________________ to come into existence

Exercise 3

Fill in each blank below with a word from the list. Each word is used only once.

ambiguous	emerged	orientation
arbitrarily	extent	prescribe
comprehensive	hierarchical	rationally
constituted	network	shortcomings
distribution		

The term "bureaucracy" is an ______________ one. It usually refers to a group of people concerned with organization and management. People often associate this term with government officials, but bureaucracy functions in the private sector of society as well. Bureaucracy is often referred to in a derogatory manner because of the frequent ______________ in administrative performance. Bureaucracies can be ______________ operated, or they can conduct themselves ______________. Some are corrupt, while others are honest. Both specialists and administrators can ______________ bureaucracies. The political ______________ of a bureaucracy as well as its status in society can vary a great deal. Often the ______________ structure of a bureaucracy permits only a very unequal ______________ of authority.

Bureaucratization operates in both the private and public spheres, in the state as well as in society. In the opinion of many, bureaucracy removes direct contact between people. Human relations become mediated, to a large ______________, by third parties, who ______________ people's behavior. This has ______________ as a ______________ process in modern society. Almost every aspect of life has become surrounded by a huge organizational ______________.

WORD SKILLS

The prefix *inter-*

Example from Passage B: *inter*action (ll. 20–21)

The prefix *inter-* adds the meaning "between," "among," or "together" to words to which it is added.

Examples:	*Prefix*	+ *Stem*	= *Word*	*Meaning*
	inter	+ change	= interchange	a giving and taking between or among people
	inter	+ view	= interview	a meeting between people

Exercise 4

Write the prefixed form for the underlined word in each sentence below.

1. The agreement among the nations to give help to the poorer nations was signed at the United Nations last week.

   An ________________ agreement to give help to the poorer nations was signed at the United Nations last week.
2. An excellent giving and taking of ideas took place before the agreement.

   An excellent ________________ of ideas took place before the agreement.
3. A few disagreements took place between several persons.

   A few ________________ disagreements took place.
4. A reporter from a New York newspaper exchanged views with several United Nations representatives and wrote a report on the agreement.

   A reporter from a New York newspaper ________________ several United Nations representatives and wrote a report on the agreement.
5. The problems of too many people and economic growth are related to each other.

   The problems of too many people and economic growth are

   ________________.

DISCOURSE SKILLS

Exercise 5

In the first paragraph, the author defines the term "bureaucracy." The author mentions several characteristics of bureaucracies, but only **one** of these characteristics is a **distinguishing characteristic** that is part of the general definition of a bureaucracy.

1. To what general class does the term "bureaucracy" belong?

   ____

2. What is a characteristic of this group?

    ____

3. What is the characteristic of a group to which the term is sometimes limited?

    ____

4. What other characteristic of bureaucracies does the author mention?

    ____

5. List three characteristics of bureaucracies that are given in the first paragraph.

    ____

    ____

    ____

6. Which of these characteristics is a **distinguishing characteristic** of a bureaucracy?

    ____

7. Which of these characteristics are **sometimes, but not always,** true of bureaucracies?

    ____

    ____

A *distinguishing characteristic* of a term is a characteristic that is always true or present for that term. In addition to its distinguishing characteristic, a term may have other characteristics that are only sometimes true or present.

8. Write a definition of the term "bureaucracy" based on the first paragraph.

    A bureaucracy is ______________________

    that is ______________________.

Exercise 6

In the second paragraph, the author mentions a number of characteristics that are sometimes true of bureaucracies and by which bureaucracies may differ. Some of these characteristics are positive and some are negative.

1. Fill in the blanks below, based on the second paragraph.

Aspect of Bureaucracy	Characteristics	
	Positive	Negative
a. conduct	__________	__________
b. performance	__________	__________
	__________	__________
c. character	__________	__________

2. In what other characteristics may bureaucracies sometimes differ?

____

____

____

3. In what way may bureaucracies function?

____

4. How may they be structured?

____

5. What statement does the author make to illustrate that bureaucracies sometimes merely serve those who are actually in control?

____

____

6. What specific example does the author cite to support this statement?

____

7. What types of differences may exist within bureaucracies?

____

____

Exercise 7

In the third paragraph, the author expands the definition of bureaucracy by defining additional distinguishing characteristics.

1. To what general class does the "bureaucratic *concept*" belong?

____

2. What is its distinguishing characteristic?

____

3. Using the definition of "bureaucracy" from Exercise 5, write a definition of "bureaucratic *concept.*"

   The bureaucratic concept is a ______________________________

   that ______________________________.

4. To what general class does the term "bureaucratization" belong?

   ____

5. In what areas may this process sometimes operate?

   ____

   ____

   ____

   ____

6. What type of human relations is characteristic of the process of bureaucratization?

   ____

7. Write a definition for the term "bureaucratization."

   Bureaucratization is ______________________________ in which

   ______________________________.

8. To what general class does the term "mediated relation" belong?

   ____

9. What is the distinguishing characteristic of this term?

   ____

   ____

10. What kinds of functionaries sometimes act as third parties?

    ____

    ____

11. Write a definition for the term "mediated relation."

    A mediated relation is ______________________________

    in which ______________________________.

12. Look back at the definition of "bureaucratic concept" (question 3). What type of human relations characterizes the system of social interactions in a bureaucracy?

    ____

13. Now write a definition of bureaucracy that includes all the distinguishing characteristics mentioned in the passage.

 A bureaucracy is ______________________________

 in which the ______________________________

 is characterized by relations in which

 ______________________________.

READING EXERCISE

Read the following passage and then do the exercises that follow.

The negative factors in a bureaucratic system are seen in the way it conducts its business, which has been described as "the disease of bureaucracy." The fundamental difficulty does not stem from its "superfluous," but from its "indispensable," aspects. Bureaucracy holds disintegrated society together. The nature and history of the bureaucratic system have to be studied so we can understand the interpersonal relationships which it forms. After all, the administrative bureaucracy itself complains about its "superfluous" aspects and the "disease of bureaucracy" and wants to rationalize its organization.

Whether the "disease" is curable, whether it is part of the system, whether indispensable bureaucracy must always include superfluous administration are by no means unimportant questions to which varied answers can be given. There are many examples which illustrate how bureaucracy wastes funds and promotes the selection of mediocrities. However, there is also evidence that modern offices function more efficiently than they did in the past; electronic machinery has replaced red tape, and the efficiency of many skilled administrative officials is noticeable. What is apparently evident in intrabureaucratic relationships, and in relationships between administrators and those they administer, is considerable "dysfunction." This "dysfunction" is inherent in bureaucracy, but it is only one of the many difficulties connected with it, and not even the essential one.

Adapted from Henry Jacoby, 1973

Exercise 8

In each blank below, write the word from the Reading Exercise passage that has nearly the same meaning as the **boldface** word or phrase in the sentence.

1. Bureaucracy has become an **absolutely essential** part of modern society.

 ____

2. There are many ways in which bureaucracies can utilize **money that is available.**

 ____

3. One problem with bureaucratic administration is that it tends to promote **those who have only ordinary ability.**

 ____

4. Bureaucracies are often characterized by **excessive attention to rules and regulations.**

 ____

5. One of the functions of bureaucracy is to hold together a society that is **separated into different parts.**

 ____

6. There is a potential conflict between the bureaucratic process and democratic values, which **is a result of** the fact that it is essential to society.

 ____

7. It is not clear whether or not bureaucracies must always include administration that is **extra and unnecessary.**

 ____

8. There is considerable **faulty functioning** in the relationships between administrators and those they administer.

 ____

9. It is apparent that various negative aspects exist as **natural and permanent** characteristics in bureaucracies.

 ____

Exercise 9

Answer the following questions based on the Reading Exercise passage.

1. What does the term "the disease of bureaucracy" describe?

 ____

2. What aspect of bureaucracy causes its fundamental difficulty?

 ____

3. Why is it necessary to study the nature and history of the bureaucratic system?

 ____

4. What three important questions does the author mention in the second paragraph?

____

____

____

5. In what ways are modern bureaucracies more efficient than those of the past?

____

____

6. What difficulty characterizes the relationships between bureaucracies?

____

7. How important a problem is this?

____

8. Does the author believe that "the disease of bureaucracy" can be cured?

____

Lesson 17

Inflation, Deflation, and the Redistribution of Income

PREREADING ACTIVITIES

A. Discussion Questions

1. How do rapidly increasing prices and costs affect your standard of living?
2. Do you think everyone is affected in the same way?
3. What people might benefit from rapidly rising prices?
4. What people might suffer from rapidly rising prices?
5. How would these people be affected by rapidly *falling* prices and costs?
6. How might rapidly rising or falling prices and costs affect the relative incomes of different people?

B. Special Vocabulary (Marked "*" in Passage A)

mortgage	a temporary and conditional promise of property to a creditor as security for the payment of a debt or loan
real estate	immovable property, such as land or buildings
overhead	the operating expenses of a business
hoarder	a person who gathers and keeps money or valuable goods hidden for future use
outlay	the amount of money spent

C. Guide Questions

As you read Passage A, ask yourself the following questions.

1. What two terms are defined in the first paragraph?
2. What happens during a time of inflation?
3. What types of people are favored by inflation?
4. Why can someone who loans money lose during a time of inflation?
5. Why do businesspersons benefit from inflation?
6. What types of people are favored by deflation?
7. Why can a merchant lose during a time of deflation?
8. Why does a schoolteacher with a fixed salary benefit from deflation?
9. What group of people tends to lose the most from inflation?

NOW READ PASSAGE A. WHEN YOU FINISH READING, ANSWER THE GUIDE QUESTIONS.

READING PASSAGES

Inflation, Deflation, and the Redistribution of Income

Adapted from Paul A. Samuelson, 1970

Passage A

Before discussing the effects of inflation and deflation on the distribution of income, it will be useful to define these terms. By *inflation* we mean a time of generally rising prices for goods and factors of production, such as **payments for work** and **money paid for the use of buildings or land.** By *deflation* we mean a time when most prices and costs are falling. Neither in inflation nor in deflation do prices all move in the same direction or in exactly the same proportion. As a result of changes in *relative* prices and in total spending, the two processes of inflation and deflation cause **clearly defined** and **typical** changes in the distribution of income among economic classes.

Inflation which is **not expected** tends to favor debtors and profit receivers at the expense of creditors and receivers of **income which does not change.** Suppose, for example, that you lend $1,000 to someone today and are paid back one year from now. If, in the **time between** when you lend the money and when you are paid back, prices have doubled, then your debtor will be paying back only one-half as much real purchasing power as you gave him. Or consider an American who was earning a fixed rate of 6 percent yearly on a *mortgage **before** World War II. This war caused a high rate of inflation in the

United States. This person found that as a result of inflation, he was not even **maintaining his position, with regard** to the real purchasing power of the dollar.

In contrast, one who invests in *real estate, in common stocks, or in **goods** makes a great money profit during times of unexpected inflation. During such times, the volume of business sales increases greatly, as do prices, between the time that businesspersons buy and sell their **products.** Fixed or *overhead costs **stay** the same; other costs rise, but not so rapidly as prices. For all these reasons, profits increase—often faster than the cost of living.

In time of deflation, the situation is the **opposite.** Creditors and receivers of income which is fixed tend to gain at the expense of debtors and profit receivers. If prices fall between the time that a creditor lends money and is repaid, then he gets back more purchasing power than he lent. Between the time that a merchant buys and sells goods, he will have to take a loss. The schoolteacher who keeps his job and whose pay is not cut, however, finds that his real income has increased. Likewise, a *hoarder, who earns no interest on the money she keeps hidden, finds that the real value of her wealth increases every day. If prices fall at the rate of 10 percent a year, she is being rewarded for her act **against society** at a 10 percent rate of interest in real terms, while the businessperson who gives someone a job may find that he cannot even get back his *outlay, much less earn a profit.

Modern research suggests that the greatest redistribution of income resulting from inflation is from older people to younger people. This is because the dollars one saves at age 25 for **the time when one can give up one's work** at age 70 often **grow smaller** in purchasing power.

NOW GO BACK AND ANSWER THE GUIDE QUESTIONS.

Passage B

Before discussing the effects of deflation and inflation on the distribution of income, it will be useful to define these terms. By *inflation* we mean a time of generally rising prices for goods and factors of production, such as **wages** and **rents.** By *deflation* we mean a time when most prices and costs are falling. Neither in inflation nor in deflation do prices all move in the same direction or in exactly the same proportion. As a result of changes in *relative* prices and in total spending, the two processes of inflation and deflation cause **definite** and **characteristic** changes in the distribution of income among economic classes.

Unforeseen inflation tends to favor debtors and profit receivers at the expense of creditors and **fixed-income** receivers. Suppose, for example, you lend $1,000 today and are paid back one year from now. If in the **meantime** prices have doubled, then your debtor will be paying back only one-half as much real purchasing power as you gave him. Or consider an American who was earning a fixed rate of 6 percent yearly on a mortgage **prior to** World War II. After 1939, he found that, as a result of inflation caused by World War II, he was not even **holding his own as far as** real purchasing power of the dollar **was concerned.**

On the other hand, one who invests in real estate, in common stocks, or in **commodities** makes a great money profit during times of unforeseen inflation, when the volume of business sales increases greatly, as do prices, between the time that businesspersons buy and sell their **merchandise.** Fixed or overhead costs **remain** the same; other costs rise, but not so rapidly as prices. For all these reasons, profits increase—often faster than the cost of living.

In time of deflation, the situation is **reversed.** Creditors and fixed-income receivers tend to gain at the expense of debtors and profit receivers. If prices fall between the time that a creditor lends money and is repaid, then he gets back more purchasing power than he lent. Between the time that a merchant buys and sells goods, he will have to take a loss. The schoolteacher who keeps his job and whose pay is not cut, however, finds that his real income has increased. Likewise, a hoarder who earns no interest on the money she keeps hidden finds the real value of her wealth increasing every day as prices fall. If prices fall at the rate of 10 percent a year, she is being rewarded for her **antisocial** act of hoarding at a 10 percent rate of interest in real terms, while the businessperson who gives someone a job may find that he cannot even get back his outlay, much less earn a profit.

Modern research suggests that the greatest redistribution of income resulting from inflation is from older people to younger people. This is because the dollars one saves at age 25 for **retirement** at age 70 often **shrink** in purchasing power.

COMPREHENSION EXERCISES

Exercise 1

Reread Passage B and then answer the following questions.

1. What is the distinguishing characteristic of the term *inflation?*

 ____

2. What is the distinguishing characteristic of the term *deflation?*

 ____

3. What two kinds of people benefit from inflation?

 ____

 ____

4. What two kinds of people lose from inflation?

____

____

5. What two examples are given in the second paragraph?

____

____

6. What effect of inflation do these examples illustrate?

____

7. What three kinds of people are given as examples in the third paragraph?

____

____

____

8. What effect of inflation do these examples illustrate?

____

9. What kinds of people benefit from deflation?

____

____

10. What kinds of people lose from deflation?

____

____

11. What two examples in the fourth paragraph illustrate people who gain from deflation?

____

____

12. What two examples illustrate people who lose from deflation?

____

____

13. Why do older people tend to lose the most from inflation?

____

Exercise 2

Complete the following charts, referring to Passage B and to your answers in Exercise 1.

During Inflation

	Types of People	Examples
Benefit		
Lose		

During Deflation

	Types of People	Examples
Benefit		
Lose		

VOCABULARY EXERCISES

Exercise 3

In each blank below, write the word from the list that best matches the definition.

commodities	remain	reversed
meantime	rent	shrink
merchandise	retirement	wages
prior to		

1. ______________________ payment for work or services
2. ______________________ time between one event and another
3. ______________________ articles or goods of trade that can be transported
4. ______________________ continue in the same condition or position
5. ______________________ to become less in amount or value
6. ______________________ money paid for the use of property
7. ______________________ products or goods that may be bought and sold
8. ______________________ in the opposite direction or position (also a verb: to move in the opposite direction)
9. ______________________ the condition of having given up one's work
10. ______________________ before

Exercise 4

Fill in each blank below with a word from the list. Each word is used only once.

commodities	remain	reversed
meantime	rents	shrinks
merchandise	retirement	wages
prior to		

During time of inflation, production costs such as ______________________ and ______________________ generally increase. Fixed costs, on the other hand, generally ______________________ the same or increase only slightly. For these reasons, people who invest in ______________________ benefit greatly from inflation. Suppose you buy 1,000 bushels of wheat tomorrow and then sell them six months from now. If in the ______________________ prices have increased 10 percent, you will make a 10 percent profit in real purchasing power, even if you sell the wheat for the same dollar amount you paid for it. Likewise with merchants, who may benefit if prices increase ______________________ the time they sell their ______________________. For persons saving for ______________________, however, the situation is ______________________, since the value of their dollars ______________________ as prices increase.

WORD SKILLS

The prefix *anti-*

Example from Passage B: *anti*social (l. 33)

The prefix *anti-* is usually added to nouns or adjectives to form adjectives. It means "against" or "in opposition to".

Examples: *Word*	*Meaning*
antifreeze	a liquid used to prevent freezing
antiwar	against war

Exercise 5

Add the prefix *anti-* to the following words and then write the new words in the correct blanks below.

freeze	smoking	war
slavery	social	

1. A group of businesspersons who are interested in promoting good health paid for an ______________________ advertisement in the local newspaper.
2. Many people feel that war is not a solution to world problems and have strong ______________________ opinions.
3. In cold climates, it is necessary to put ______________________ into car engines during the winter.

4. The strong ____________________ feelings of many Americans eventually led to the freeing of slaves in America in the late nineteenth century.
5. Some people find it difficult to make friends because of their

   ____________________ behavior.

DISCOURSE SKILLS

Exercise 6

Reread Passage B and then answer the following questions.

Paragraph 1

1. What happens to prices and factors of production during inflation?

   ____

2. What happens to prices and factors of production during deflation?

   ____

3. Do all prices move in the same direction and by the same proportion during inflation and deflation?

   ____

4. In general, what happens to relative prices and total spending during both inflation and deflation?

   ____

5. What changes do the processes of inflation and deflation cause?

   ____

6. What characteristic of inflation and deflation are these changes a result of?

   ____

Paragraph 2

7. Suppose you lend $1,000 to someone and are paid back in one year. What will happen to the purchasing power of your money if in the meantime prices double?

   ____

8. Did World War II cause inflation or deflation?

   ____

9. What happened to the purchasing power of the mortgage holder's dollar because of this inflation?

____

Paragraph 3

10. What happens to the volume of business during inflation?

____

11. What happens to prices?

____

12. What happens to costs?

fixed or overhead costs ___________________________

other costs ___________________________

13. For what reasons do profits increase during inflation?

____

____

____

Paragraph 4

14. What happens to a creditor's purchasing power if prices fall between the time he lends money and is repaid?

____

15. What happens to the real value of a hoarder's money if prices fall?

____

Paragraph 5

16. What causes the redistribution of income from older people to younger people?

____

17. Why does this happen?

____

A *causal relationship* is one in which one event, condition, or factor comes ahead of another in time and in which the first event, condition, or factor causes a change in the second. A *causal construction* is used to express a causal relationship. It consists of three components:

1. **an event, condition, or factor that is the *cause* (more than one event, condition or factor may be the cause)**
2. **an event or condition that is the *effect* (more than one event or condition may be the effect)**
3. **the *marker* of the causal construction.**

Examples: The two processes of inflation and deflation (Cause) cause (Marker) definite and characteristic changes . . . (Effect)

If (Marker) prices fall at the rate of 10 percent a year, (Cause) she is being rewarded . . . at a 10 percent rate of interest. (Effect)

Verbs and verb phrases such as *cause, result in, result from, affect,* and *have an effect on* can function as markers of causal constructions. *Cause* and *result in* are used to indicate a specific effect. *Affect* and *have an effect on* are used simply to indicate that there is a causal relationship between the two events or conditions.

Examples: World War II (Cause) *caused* (Marker) prices to rise in the United States (Effect)

World War II (Cause) *resulted in* (Marker) a rise in prices in the United States (Effect)

A rise in prices in the United States (Effect) *resulted from* (Marker) World War II. (Cause)

Note: With the verb phrase "result *from*," the **effect** is stated first.

Inflation and deflation (Cause) *affect* (Marker) the distribution of income. (Effect)

Inflation and deflation (Cause) *have an effect on* (Marker) . . . income. (Effect)

Exercise 7

In each of the following sentences, underline the **cause,** draw two lines under the **effect,** and circle the words that are the **marker** of the causal construction.

1. Inflation and deflation have an effect on the distribution of income among economic classes.
2. Inflation results in benefits to debtors and profit receivers.
3. Fixed costs and increasing prices have an effect on profits.
4. Inflation results in the redistribution of income from older to younger people.
5. Changes in relative prices and total spending result in definite and characteristic changes in the distribution of income among economic classes.
6. Deflation affects both debtors and creditors.
7. Inflation was caused by World War II.
8. Deflation results in an increase in real purchasing power for fixed-income receivers.
9. Increased sales, along with rising prices and fixed costs, cause profits to increase during times of inflation.
10. Unforeseen inflation affects debtors and creditors differently.

Some markers of causal constructions come immediately before the *cause:*
IF BECAUSE (OF) DUE TO AS A RESULT OF

Examples: *If* prices fall . . . *then* he gets back more . . .
Marker Cause Marker Effect

He gets back more . . . *if* prices fall.
Effect Marker Cause

As a result of inflation . . . he was not even holding his own.
Marker Cause Effect

He was not even holding his own, *as a result of* inflation.
Effect Marker Cause

This is *because* the dollars one saves . . . often shrink.
Effect Marker Cause

Because the dollars one saves . . . often shrink,
Marker Cause

the greatest redistribution is from older people to younger.

Effect

Increases in profits are *due to* rising prices and stable costs.

Effect Marker Cause

Due to rising prices and stable costs, profits are increasing.

Marker Cause Effect

Exercise 8

In each of the following sentences, underline the **cause,** draw two lines under the **effect,** and circle the words that are the **marker** of the causal construction.

1. There was a period of inflation during World War II, and as a result, holders of fixed mortgages suffered losses in real purchasing power.
2. Due to the increased cost of housing in the past few years, many people can no longer afford to purchase homes.
3. There has been an increase in the price of fresh vegetables because of the severely cold weather.
4. If the cost of wages goes up, then it will be necessary to raise the price of our products.
5. The price of gasoline has fallen slightly because of the large supply on the market.
6. The rise in the cost of building materials in the past six months was a result of the increase in the amount of lumber needed for building.
7. The recent increase in unemployment is largely due to cutbacks by manufacturers in production.
8. Many people will not be able to buy new homes if interest rates continue to increase.
9. The price of syrup doubled during World War I. As a result, the Wilson Bottling Company discontinued bottling "Cheer-Up."
10. Some economists expect interest rates to continue increasing until the

end of the year. If this happens, the value of the dollar against foreign currencies is also likely to rise.

Some markers of causal constructions come immediately before the *effect:*
THEN FOR THIS REASON CONSEQUENTLY AS A RESULT

Examples: *If* . . . prices have doubled, *then*

Marker Cause Marker

your debtor will be paying back only one-half. . .

Effect

For all these reasons profits increase.

Marker Effect

The dollars one saves . . . often shrink in purchasing power.

Cause

Consequently, income is redistributed . . .

Marker Effect

Relative prices change during inflation and deflation, and

Cause

as a result, there are changes in the distribution of income.

Marker Effect

Exercise 9

In each of the following sentences, underline the **cause,** draw two lines under the **effect,** and circle the words that are the **marker** of the causal construction.

1. The cost of steel rose steeply during the first quarter. For this reason, the company delayed production of all new models until the next quarter.
2. The construction of new homes has increased in the past six months, and consequently many more workers have been able to find jobs.
3. If the factory cannot meet its production needs, then it will be necessary to hire more workers.

4. Annual profits were down by 15 percent. Consequently, the company was not able to pay its stockholders a dividend this year.
5. We have been able to reduce our costs by nearly 10 percent by careful budgeting. As a result, it will be possible for us to expand operations in the coming months.

READING EXERCISE

Read the following passage and then do the exercises that follow.

In addition to redistributing incomes, inflation may affect the total real income and production of the community. An increase in prices is usually associated with high employment. In moderate inflation, industries are operating efficiently and output is near capacity. There is a great deal of private investment and jobs are plentiful. Such has been the historical pattern. Thus, many businesspersons and union leaders, in evaluating a little deflation and a little inflation, consider the latter to be the lesser of two evils. In mild inflation, the losses to fixed-income groups are usually less than the gains to the rest of the community. Even workers with relatively fixed wages are often better off because of improved employment opportunities and greater take-home pay, a rise in interest rates on new securities may partly compensate for any losses to creditors, and increases in pension benefits may partly make up losses to retirees.

In deflation, on the other hand, the growing unemployment of labor and capital causes the community's total well-being to be less; so, in a sense, the gainers get less than the losers lose. As a matter of fact, in a depression, or a time of severe deflation, almost everyone suffers, including the creditor who is left with uncollectable debts.

For these reasons an increase in consumption of investment spending is considered good in times of unemployment, even if this tends to increase prices slightly. When the economic system is suffering from severe depression, few people will criticize private or public spending on the ground that this might be inflationary. Actually, most of this increased spending will increase production and create jobs. Once full employment and full plant capacity have been reached, however, any further increases in spending are likely to be completely wasted in price increases.

Adapted from Paul A. Samuelson, 1970

Exercise 10

In each blank below, write the word from the Reading Exercise passage that has nearly the same meaning as the **boldface** word or phrase in the sentence preceding.

1. Before reaching a decision, it is necessary to **determine the value** of all the different alternatives.

   ____

2. The insurance company **paid** the workers **to make up for** their lost wages while the factory was being rebuilt after the fire.

   ____

3. People who invest in **stocks and bonds** may suffer losses during a time of deflation.

   ____

4. The plant is operating at its **highest possible level of production.**

   ____

5. When there is **not an excessive amount** of inflation, workers are generally better off than during times of deflation.

   ____

6. During **extreme** depression, investment spending tends to increase production.

   ____

7. It is quite common for the government and employers to increase **the money paid as a retirement benefit** during times of inflation.

   ____

8. An increase in the **amount** of investment spending **used** is considered good when there is high unemployment.

   ____

Exercise 11

Answer the following questions, based on the Reading Exercise passage.

1. What two things are affected by inflation?

   ____

   ____

2. What are four characteristics of industries during times of moderate inflation?

 ____

 ____

 ____

 ____

3. Which do businesspersons and union leaders prefer, a little inflation or a little deflation?

 ____

4. For what two reasons are workers on fixed wages generally better off during a time of moderate inflation than during a time of moderate deflation?

 ____

 ____

5. What characteristic of deflation causes the community as a whole to be less well-off?

 ____

6. What are three effects of an increase in investment spending?

 ____

 ____

 ____

7. At what point are spending increases no longer beneficial?

 ____

Lesson 18

The Consequences of Rapid Population Growth

PREREADING ACTIVITIES

A. Discussion Questions

1. What factors cause the population of a country to decrease?
2. What factors cause the population of a country to increase?
3. What types of countries tend to have the highest rates of population growth?
4. How does a rapidly increasing population affect the economy of a country?
5. What are some nonbeneficial effects of increases in population?
6. What are some beneficial effects of increases in population?
7. What would happen if the population stabilized?

B. Special Vocabulary (Marked "*" in Passage A)

gross national product	the sum of all the goods and services produced and the increases in investments in a country for one year
subsist	to exist
diet	the food and drink usually eaten
upheaval	a violent change

inherit	to receive property from someone, usually one's parents, and usually when they die
siblings	two or more persons having the same parents

C. Guide Questions

As you read Passage A, ask yourself the following questions.

1. What kinds of nations are experiencing the highest rates of population growth?
2. What happens to any economic advances as a result of rapid population growth?
3. What happens to jobs if population growth is much greater than the growth of the economy?
4. What might be the result of low income, few jobs, and many people living in cities?
5. What happens to the average age of people when there is rapid population growth?
6. What causes this to happen?
7. What kinds of problems occur in agricultural societies with rapidly increasing populations?

NOW READ PASSAGE A. WHEN YOU FINISH READING, ANSWER THE GUIDE QUESTIONS.

READING PASSAGES

The Consequences of Rapid Population Growth

Adapted from Dressler and Carns, 1973

Passage A

Many countries are experiencing population growth rates of 3 to 4 percent per year, which means that their populations will double very quickly. The nations that are experiencing the highest rates of natural increase are almost entirely those in the economically "developing" or "underdeveloped" categories.

One of the most **easily seen nonbeneficial results** of rapid population growth is that **any** economic advances that are being made in the society as a whole are **reduced to nothing** by the addition of people. If a developing country manages to increase its *gross national product by 1 or 2 percent a year but experiences a 3 or 4 percent population growth rate at the same time, the **final** result is that per capita income and wealth decline. Since income is unequally distributed in **practically** all societies, and since the societies **concerned** are relatively poor to begin with, this means that increasing numbers of people starve, live **very close to** starvation, or **barely** exist, surviving only from day to day. Exact statistics are difficult to **obtain.** However, it is clear that a large proportion of the populations in many nations are actually starving or *subsisting on inadequate *diets.

A second result, which is **associated** with the first, is that a large **part** of the population is either **not employed** or is **only partly employed.** For if the rate of population increase **is** much **greater than** the growth of the economy, the proportion of people who are without employment must rise.

Under the **specific** conditions of low per capita income, people having no work, and the **gathering** of people in urban areas, the potential for political instability is great. This does not mean that revolutions are necessarily a *bad* result of population growth. Political *upheavals of this type may reflect the **disappointments caused** by low quality of life. However, they may not result in meaningful redistributions of power, privilege, and income within a society or lead to a **large** reduction in the rate of natural population increase.

A fourth result of rapid population growth may be harder to **understand.** When a population is increasing **because** of relatively high birth rates and a markedly declining death rate, it becomes significantly younger. For example, if a nation's annual growth rate is 4 percent, approximately half the population will be 15 years of age or younger. In the United States, with its low death rate but somewhat higher birth rate, the **average** age is in the mid-20s.

The **occurrence** of this process is due to population's changing from the bottom up—that is, younger age groups increase or decrease in numbers more rapidly and at an earlier date than do older age groups. Greater proportions of children lead to other problems, of course. Additional **buildings, equipment,** and **materials** for education are needed; there are fewer places in the economy unless it is **growing rapidly;** and a shortage of jobs leads to political unrest, poverty, and a lowered quality of life. **In addition,** in agricultural societies, greater proportions of children lead to two kinds of **problems: between** different **age levels within the family,** such as between parents and children, and **within** the same age level, such as among children. The former are due to the fact that children must wait longer to *inherit the family's property, while the latter are the result of greater competition among *siblings.

NOW GO BACK AND ANSWER THE GUIDE QUESTIONS

Passage B

Many countries are experiencing growth rates of 3 to 4 percent per year, which means that their populations will double very quickly. The nations that are experiencing the highest rates of natural increase are almost entirely those in the economically "developing" or "underdeveloped" categories.

One of the most **obvious negative consequences** of rapid population growth is that **whatever** economic advances are being made in the society as a whole are **canceled** by the addition of people. If a developing country manages to increase its gross national product by 1 or 2 percent a year but experiences at the same time a 3 or 4 percent population growth rate, the **net** result is that per capita income and wealth decline. Since income is unequally distributed in **virtually** all societies, and since the societies **in question** are relatively poor to begin with, this means that increasing numbers of people starve, live **at the edge of** starvation, or exist **marginally,** on a day-to-day basis for survival. Exact statistics on starvation are difficult to **secure.** However, it is clear that a large proportion of the populations in many nations are actually starving or subsisting on inadequate diets.

A second and **related** consequence is **unemployment** and **underemployment** for a large **segment** of the population. For if the rate of population increase greatly **exceeds** the growth of the economy, the unemployment rate must rise.

Under **given** conditions of low per capita income, unemployment, and urban **concentration,** the potential for political instability is great. This does not mean that revolutions are necessarily a *negative* consequence of population growth. But although political upheavals of this type may reflect the **frustrations generated** by a low quality of life, they may not result in meaningful redistributions of power, privilege, and income within society or lead to a **substantial** reduction in the rate of natural population increase.

A fourth consequence of rapid population growth may be harder to **grasp.** When a population is increasing **as a function** of relatively high birth rates and a markedly declining death rate, it becomes significantly younger. For example, if a nation's annual growth rate is 4 percent, approximately half the population will be 15 years of age or younger. In the United States, with its low death rate but somewhat higher birth rate, the **median** age is in the mid-20s.

This **phenomenon** is due to population's changing from the bottom up—that is, younger age groups increase or decrease in numbers more rapidly and at an earlier date than do older age groups. Greater proportions of children lead to other problems, of course. Additional educational **facilities** are needed; there are fewer places in the economy unless it is **booming,** and a shortage of jobs leads to political unrest, poverty, and a lowered quality of life. **Moreover,** in agricultural societies, greater proportions of children lead to both ***inter*generational** and ***intra*generational stresses.** The former are due to the fact that children must wait a longer time to inherit the family's holdings, while the latter are a result of greater competition among siblings.

COMPREHENSION EXERCISE

Exercise 1

Reread Passage B and then answer the following questions.

Paragraph 1

1. What is one characteristic of most countries that are categorized as "developing" or "underdeveloped"?

____

Paragraph 2

2. What generalization is made about one consequence of rapid population growth?

____

3. What example is given to illustrate this generalization?

____

4. Is this an actual or a hypothetical example (see Lesson 7)?

____

5. In a society with unequal distribution of income, will everyone be rich or poor?

____

6. To what kind of societies does the phrase "societies in question" (l. 11) refer?

____

Paragraph 3

7. What two words are used to refer to a lack of sufficient work?

____

____

8. What would happen to the unemployment rate if economic growth exceeded population growth?

____

Paragraph 4

9. To what does the phrase "of this type" (l. 24) refer?

____

10. To what does the word "they" (l. 25) refer?

____

11. What three terms are used in this paragraph to refer to the temporary breakdown and violent change in the system of government?

    ______________________, ______________________,

    ____

12. What three conditions are characteristic of a low quality of life?

    ______________________, ______________________,

    ____

Paragraph 5

13. What generalization is made in the second sentence?

    ____

14. What hypothetical example is given to illustrate this generalization?

    ____

    ____

15. What actual example is given to illustrate this generalization?

    ____

Paragraph 6

16. To what does the phrase "this phenomenon" (l. 34) refer?

    ____

17. What two groups are compared in the first sentence?

    ____

    ____

18. What characteristic is the criterion of this comparison?

    ____

19. What two phrases are used to mean a lack of sufficient work?

    ____

    ____

20. What two kinds of stresses are contrasted in the last paragraph?

    ____

    ____

21. In what way are these two types of stresses different?

    ____

22. What leads to intergenerational stresses?

____

____

23. What causes intragenerational stresses?

____

VOCABULARY EXERCISES

Exercise 2

In each blank below, write the word from the list that best matches the definition.

consequence	generation	phenomenon
exceed	marginal	segment
facilities	obvious	virtually
generate		

1. ________________ part or section
2. ________________ to be greater than
3. ________________ easily seen or understood
4. ________________ effect or result
5. ________________ in effect; essentially
6. ________________ produce; cause to exist
7. ________________ an occurrence that can be directly perceived by the senses
8. ________________ barely above the lowest acceptable level
9. ________________ a single level or stage in family descent
10. ________________ materials or services that make it easier to accomplish something

Exercise 3

Fill in each blank below with a word from the list. Some words are used more than once.

consequence(s)	generations	phenomena
exceeds	marginally	segment(s)
facilities	obvious	virtually
generate		

There are several negative ______________________ of rapid population growth. Perhaps the most ______________________ of these is the cancellation of economic advances by the addition of people. In societies that are relatively poor, which includes ______________________ all the societies with high rates of population growth, large ______________________ of the populations survive ______________________ on inadequate diets.

In countries where population growth ______________________ economic growth, unemployment results. This, along with low per capita income and urban concentration, may ______________________ political instability.

Another ______________________ of rapid population growth is a lowering of the median age of the population. This ______________________ occurs because younger age groups increase in number more rapidly than do older age groups. If a large ______________________ of the population consists of children, more educational ______________________ are needed. Rapid population growth in agricultural societies may also result in stresses both within and across ______________________.

WORD SKILLS

The prefix *under-*

Example from Passage B: *under*developed (l. 4)
*under*employment (ll. 17–18)

The prefix *under-* is added to verbs and nouns. It means "less than normal."

Examples: *Word*	*Meaning*
underpaid	paid less than the normal value
underweight	weighing less than normal

The prefix *under-* can also mean "located below or under."

Examples: *Word*	*Meaning*
underground	located under the ground
underlie	to be located under or below
undersecretary	person below the rank of secretary

Exercise 4

Add the prefix *under-* to the following words and then write the correct form of the new words in the correct blanks below.

privilege	staff	use
represent	state	value

1. Because of the unequal distribution of votes, the province was ____________ in the National Assembly.
2. The minister had very little confidence in the government and consequently ____________ its official position.
3. Due to the decrease in the market for our products, many of the facilities in the plant are ____________.
4. Dissatisfaction among the ____________ people of a society can sometimes lead to political unrest.
5. Many of our employees are either on vacation or ill, so that we are temporarily ____________.
6. The insurance appraiser was not certain how much the house was worth, and consequently ____________ it considerably.

DISCOURSE SKILLS

The markers *since* and *as a function of* come immediately before the cause, in a causal construction.

Examples: *Since* income is unequally distributed . . . ,

Marker — Cause

and *since* the societies . . . are relatively poor . . . ,

Marker — Cause

increasing numbers . . . exist marginally.
Effect

In agricultural societies there is intergenerational stress,
Effect

since children must wait longer . . .
Marker Cause

Population increases *as a function of* relatively high . . .
Effect Marker Cause

The verb *lead to* functions in the same way as *cause*.

Example: A shortage of jobs *leads to* political unrest . . .
Cause Marker Effect

Exercise 5

In each of the following sentences, underline the **cause(s),** draw two lines under the **effect(s),** and circle the words that are the **marker** of the causal construction.

1. Greater proportions of children lead to both intergenerational and intragenerational stresses.
2. There is a high rate of unemployment, since the population is increasing rapidly while the economy is remaining more or less stable.
3. Low per capita income, unemployment, and urban concentration may lead to political unrest.
4. The unemployment rate increases as a function of a high rate of population growth and a slow growth of the economy.
5. A slow increase in the gross national product, combined with a rapid increase in population, leads to a net decline in per capita income and wealth.
6. Since there are fewer places in the economy, there is considerable political unrest and poverty.

7. The proportion of children increases as a function of rapid increases in younger age groups and slower increases in older age groups.

Exercise 6

Reread Passage B and then answer the following questions.

Paragraph 2

1. What is the main consequence of rapid population growth discussed in this paragraph?

____

2. What two factors in a developing country decline if population growth exceeds the increase in the gross national product?

____

____

3. What two conditions generally characterize societies with rapid population growth?

____

____

4. What three conditions can lead to starvation or near starvation for large proportions of the populations in many nations?

____

____

____

The causal relationships described in the second paragraph can be illustrated in a diagram like the one below. In this diagram, the circles represent conditions or factors and lines with arrows (→) represent causal relationships, with the arrows pointing from the cause to the effect.

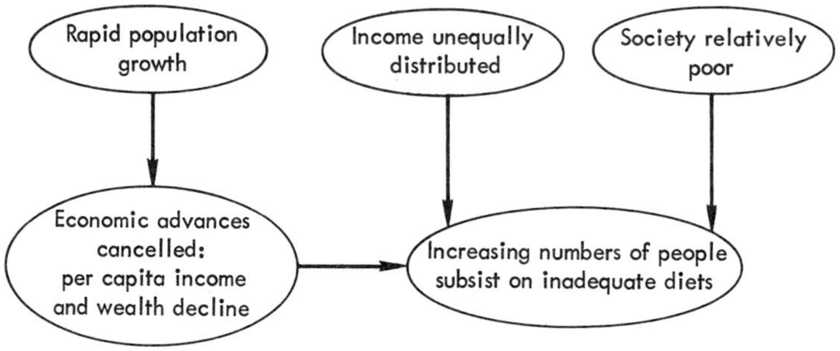

According to this diagram, there is a **direct** causal relationship between several pairs of conditions, as indicated by a single arrow between the two conditions:

rapid population growth	→	declines in per capita income and wealth
declines in per capita income and wealth }	→	inadequate diets
unequal distribution of income }	→	inadequate diets
relative poverty of society	→	inadequate diets

There is an **indirect** relationship between one pair of conditions:

rapid population growth inadequate diets

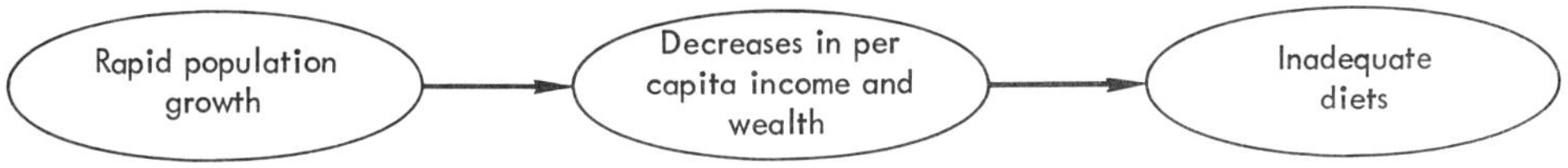

Paragraph 3

5. What consequence of rapid population growth is discussed in this paragraph?

____

____

6. Growth in what two conditions affects the unemployment rate?

____

____

7. Based on your answers to questions 5 and 6, complete the following causal diagram.

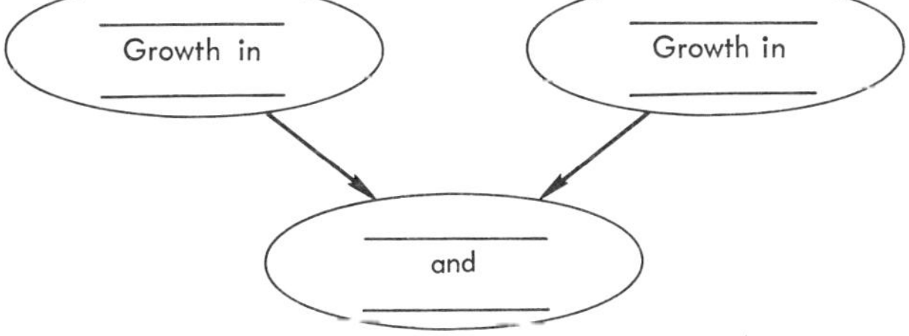

Paragraph 4

8. What consequence of rapid population growth is discussed in this paragraph?

____

9. What three conditions affect the potential for political instability?

____

____

____

10. What do these conditions, which are characteristic of a low quality of life, generate?

____

11. What beneficial effects may *not* result from revolutions?

____

____

12. Based on your answers to questions 8, 9, 10, complete the following causal diagram.

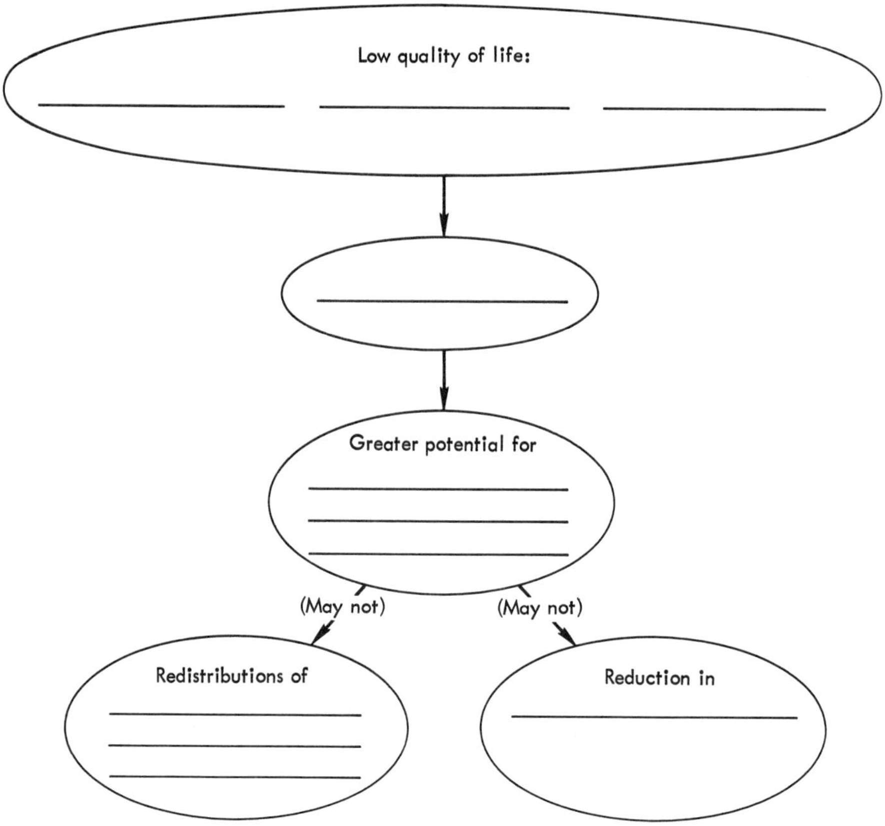

Paragraph 5

13. What is the fourth consequence of rapid population growth?

____

14. What two factors cause an increase in population?

____

____

15. Based on your answers to questions 13 and 14, complete the following causal diagram.

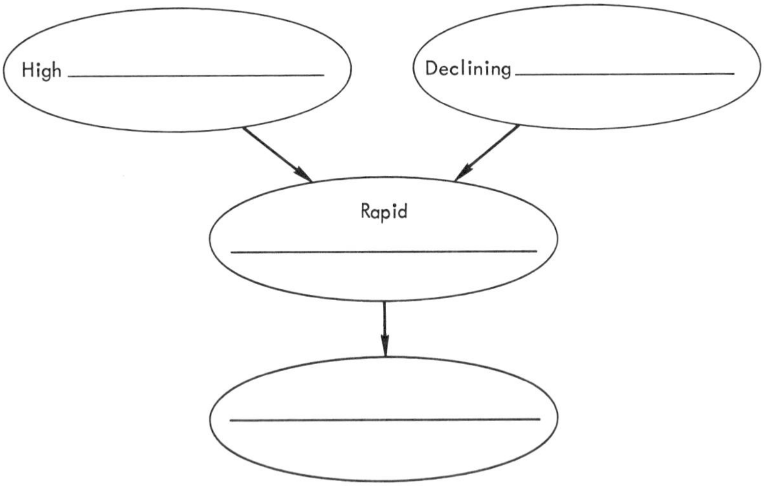

Paragraph 6

16. What two groups increase or decrease in numbers when there is rapid population growth?

____

____

17. Which group increases more rapidly?

____

18. What is the result of differing rates of increase between these two groups?

____

19. What problems are caused by increasing proportions of children?

____

____

20. What are three effects of a shortage of jobs?

____

____

____

21. In agricultural societies, what are the results of greater proportions of children?

____

____

22. What condition causes intergenerational stress?

____

23. What condition causes intragenerational stress?

____

24. Based on your answers to questions 16–23, complete the causal diagram on the following page.

READING EXERCISE

Read the following passage and then do the exercises that follow.

Two distinct patterns of population distribution may be noted in the world. A given nation will have one or the other, depending upon how economically developed it is. In rich countries, urban growth is brought about by migration from rural areas and by natural increase. Of these two factors, the first has been the most significant during the first half of the twentieth century. In poor countries, however, both rural and urban sectors are growing at very fast rates. Since rural population growth forces people off the land by creating a shortage of land to farm, and since cities have traditionally attracted people because of their presumed opportunities for a better quality of life, urban growth in many developing nations has been considerable. Thus, a consequence of overpopulation is overurbanization. This occurs when the number of people in urban areas far exceeds the long-range potential of the economy to support them. Many observers, for example, have described certain Asian cities as "teeming." And in Latin America, towns of small, poorly built houses have grown up at the edges of virtually every large city, containing migrants from rural areas who seek some advantage in the urban environment but are forced to live at or near the starvation level in unsanitary, disease-ridden conditions.

Adapted from Dressler & Carns, 1973

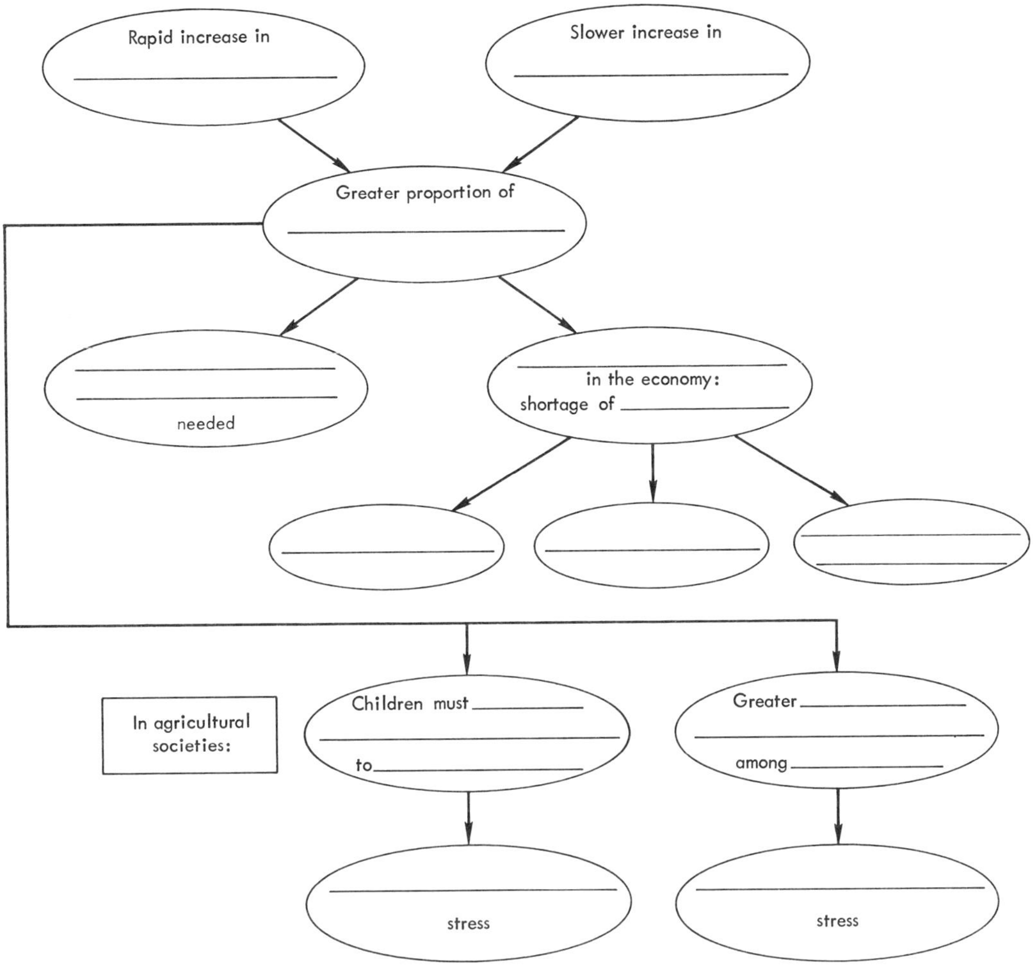

Diagram for question 24, Exercise 6.

Exercise 7

In each blank below, write the word from the Reading Exercise passage that has nearly the same meaning as the **boldface** word or phrase in the sentence.

1. Many people are **drawn toward** cities by the promise of excitement and better life.

   ____

2. Several **clearly marked** characteristics distinguish urban from rural populations.

   ____

3. The effects of bureaucratic growth can be seen in both the private and public **parts** of society.

____

4. People may move from rural areas to cities because they **suppose** that the quality of their life will improve there.

____

5. One consequence of overpopulation in rural areas is the **movement** of people to cities.

____

6. Poor people in cities may be forced to live in **unclean** conditions.

____

7. **People who move** from the country to cities are often disappointed in the quality of life they find there.

____

Exercise 8

Answer the following questions, based on the Reading Exercise passage.

1. What two patterns of population distribution are discussed?

____

____

2. What two factors result in urban growth in rich countries?

____

____

3. What causes a shortage of land in rural areas?

____

4. What happens to people as a result of this shortage of land?

____

5. Why have people traditionally been attracted to cities?

____

6. What two factors have led to the migration from rural to urban areas in poor countries?

   ____

   ____

7. How might you define overurbanization?

   ____

8. What two examples of overurbanization are given?

   ____

   ____